Alan Robinson qualified as a solicitor in 1972. He has spent the whole of his working life focussing on areas of practice around welfare law (in particular social security and community care) and around the law as it affects charities. He has written and spoken extensively on these topics. He retired from legal practice in 2010 and now works part-time as a consultant and trainer. He is the author of "*Introduction to the Law of Community Care in England and Wales*" (Law Brief Publishing).

A Practical Guide to Personal Injury Trusts – 2nd Edition

A Practical Guide to Personal Injury Trusts – 2nd Edition

Alan Robinson,
MA (York), MA (Sheffield),
LL.B (London), Solicitor

Law Brief Publishing

Published 2020 by Law Brief Publishing, an imprint of Law Brief Publishing Ltd
30 The Parks
Minehead
Somerset
TA24 8BT

www.lawbriefpublishing.com

Paperback: 978-1-912687-85-5

PREFACE TO THE SECOND EDITION

The main change since the publication of the first edition in 2016 has been the advance of universal credit as the main means tested benefit, in place of income support, housing benefit, and so on. The change to the law regarding personal injuries trusts has been minor, since the new benefit rules largely reflect the old; but if one sets out to explain something (in this case universal credit) then one must accept the obligation to explain it in sufficient detail to make sense for the reader.

Apart from this, there are changes in allocated amounts, and minor changes in detail (and correction of some errors). What there is not, and what we might have hoped for following the Care Act 2014, is some attempt to address the issue of paying for care in a comprehensive and coherent manner, so that the complexities of personal injury trusts continue to apply (in England at any rate, and also largely in Wales) to someone whose care needs are likely to be the responsibility of the local authority. It is to be hoped that the Government, or some future Government, will address this particular issue, which is the cause of much hardship and uncertainty.

One of the problems with producing work at about the end of the financial year is that tax and benefit and other rates tend to increase at that time. I have tried to say which I have used; the benefit rates are generally those applying during 2020/21, but not all of the NHS or tax rates are as readily available at the time of writing.

With that reservation, I have endeavoured to state the law at 16th March 2020.

Alan Robinson
16th March 2020

CONTENTS

Chapter One	Personal Injury Trusts: Overview and Preliminary Considerations	1
Chapter Two	Means-Tested Benefits: Principal Rules	7
Chapter Three	How Personal Injury Compensation Is Dealt With	25
Chapter Four	Non Contributory Disability Benefits	37
Chapter Five	Local Authority Services	47
Chapter Six	Paying for Care	63
Chapter Seven	NHS Continuing Health Care	85
Chapter Eight	Types of Personal Injury Trust	93
Chapter Nine	The Mentally Incapable Client and the Court of Protection	113
Chapter Ten	Problem Areas for Practitioners	127
Chapter Eleven	Conclusion and Further Resources	139
Appendix 1	Personal Independence Payments	141
Appendix 2	Employment and Support Allowance	147

CHAPTER ONE
PERSONAL INJURY TRUSTS: OVERVIEW AND PRELIMINARY CONSIDERATIONS

1.1 An Overview of Personal Injury Trusts

Personal injury trusts were originally created as a response to the capital rule in means tested social security benefits. Put simply, this rule denies certain means tested benefits to those with capital in excess of a certain amount. This then creates a problem for the existing benefit claimant who receives a sum of capital, in that he or she will on the face of it be immediately deprived of access to his or her benefits. This would be the case in the event of a windfall such as a legacy or lottery win; and this can be seen as supporting the reasoning behind the rule in the first place. The state should not support someone who has adequate resources of their own. In order for the rule to apply, the claimant must be able to gain access to the money, so that, for example, a legacy which is set out in the form of a discretionary trust will not of itself invoke the rule.

In order to prevent abuse of the rule, a person who seeks to give their capital away in order to gain access to benefits will nevertheless be caught under what is normally known as the deprivation rule. The capital they have given away becomes "notional capital" and is taken into account as if they still possessed it.

Where the rule is applied because someone becomes entitled to a sum of money as compensation for personal injury, however, the purpose of the rule is being corrupted. Personal injury compensation, by definition, is not a windfall, but is a sum of money designed to compensate for pain and suffering, and also to meet the additional costs of care which have come about as a result of the injury. The capital rule was therefore amended, initially so as to provide a limited amount of protection for the benefit claimant with personal injury compensation, and subsequently to make the idea of placing the compensation in a trust fully workable, so that it could be ignored for benefit purposes.

Originally, therefore, a personal injury trust was simply a method of sheltering the compensation paid to someone as a result of their personal injury. For someone receiving means tested benefits, this would mean that the compensation did not form part of their capital for benefit purposes, and they would therefore not be caught by the maximum capital rules. Similarly, if they were (or were likely to become) resident in residential care, the capital rules which limit the amount payable by them would be avoided by this method.

At the same time, following the coming into force of the Finance Act 2006, the merits of personal injury trusts as a device to deal with the tax implications of an award have become more apparent. It may therefore be the case that the personal injury trust needs to be employed as a method of tax planning, especially if it is desired to provide protection for the dependants of the injured person.

The term 'personal injury' is widely understood. The term covers all types of accidental and criminal injuries, and also clinical and other negligence. Almost any physical or mental harm caused to a person will be relevant.

The personal injury trust is often not just a device which benefits the person injured, and there may also be benefits for other people, which are explored further below.

In order to take advantage of the disregarding of personal injury compensation, a trust must be established. There are few formalities associated with the setting up of the trust. There is no requirement for a specific type of trust, and nor is a court order required (in most cases). It is the source of the trust fund, not the method used, which determines whether the trust can count as a personal injury trust for benefit purposes. It is not confined to private trusts, but also covers a trust arising from funds which are administered by the Court.

There is no specific time limit for setting up a trust, but if there is a delay, then the capital rule may result in the moneys being treated as capital by the Department of Work and Pensions ("DWP"), and thus in benefits being lost. Once this is done, benefits may take a long time to reinstate. It may be difficult to trace the trust back in time in order to show when a trust came into existence, and from what point the benefits disregard should start.

It is therefore recommended that the issue of a personal injury trust be raised with a client straight away, at least as far as someone presently in receipt of benefits is concerned. Time runs from the receipt of any payment, so if nothing is done, their entitlement to means tested benefits will be lost if the trust rules are not complied with; and even if they are, time will start running from receipt of the first payment.

A claimant has a duty to inform the DWP, or the local authority (as appropriate), of any relevant 'change of circumstances' which includes an increase in personal capital. This covers DWP benefits such as income support, income related employment and support allowance, income based jobseekers allowance, universal credit, and pension credit; and local authority benefits such as housing benefit. It will also apply to local authority-funded services such as residential care.

The duty, under Section 111A of the **Social Security Administration Act 1992** as inserted by the **Social Security Fraud Act 2001**, is to make a 'prompt' notification. A client who does not notify is not only likely to be required to repay any benefit overpaid as a result of the failure. They are also liable to prosecution under the Act. This means that the client is potentially committing a criminal offence by failing to notify, and therefore a duty may fall on any solicitor involved to complete a referral to the National Crime Agency.

This book firstly looks at the different benefits, setting out how they approach questions of personal injury compensation; it them considers other possible care needs and how the receipt of compensation will affect them – local authority care, and continuing NHS health care. We then consider the different types of trusts, and some of the problems which they may raise for the practitioner.

1.2 Creating a Trust: Introduction

In principle any type of trust may form a personal injury trust. It is the source of the funds, not the type of trust, which determines entitlement to the exemption for benefit purposes.

However, this situation was affected by the **Finance Act 2006**, which means that there may also be tax implications for certain types of trust. The **Finance Act 2006** amended the **Inheritance Tax Act 1984** in respect of trusts founded after 21st March 2006.

Although it may be desirable that the only factors determining the question of whether there should be a trust at all, and its type, are those of personal and family needs, this will now only be the case where compensation does not exceed the injured party's 'nil rate band' (the level above which inheritance tax can be charged). At present this is £325,000, less any chargeable lifetime transfers during the previous seven years. A transfer of value into most forms of trust which exceeds that amount will now trigger an immediate inheritance tax charge at the lifetime rate (20%), and may incur further charges.

In order to avoid this, it is therefore necessary to consider the tax implications of the form of trust chosen.

The different forms of trust are considered in outline in chapter 8 below.

1.3 Underlying considerations

Different trusts are set up for different purposes, and give different rights and responsibilities to the trustees and the beneficiary. Although it is noted above that the type of trust does not matter when considering benefit protection, there may be additional or different motivations which clients have when setting up a personal injury trust. Some examples are:-

- They may wish to preserve their entitlement to means tested benefits. This may also apply to their family after their death.
- They may be nervous about handling a large sum of money, of which they have had no previous experience.
- There may be an instance of mental ill health, or even lack of capacity, which may require the presence of trustees.
- They may wish to shelter their money against predatory relatives.
- They may not wish the 'hassle' of handling the money and may just wish to get on with their lives.
- There may be a risk of divorce or separation and a wish to exclude any compensation from inclusion in any matrimonial settlement.

We first consider the benefit rules and how they deal with a personal injury trust.

CHAPTER TWO
MEANS-TESTED BENEFITS: PRINCIPAL RULES

At the time of writing, the benefit system is in transition from providing several benefits to providing a single means tested benefit for people of working age. The new benefit is universal credit. This is being phased in across the country, so that (broadly speaking) new claims for means tested benefits are treated as being made for universal credit, but people on continuing claims which began before the date of its implementation will in many cases continue to receive one or more of the "legacy" benefits which universal credit is replacing. Part One of this chapter therefore covers the position in those areas where universal credit is already in place, and Part Two covers those areas where the transfer to universal credit is not complete and claimants are likely to be receiving one or more of the legacy benefits. It is therefore necessary initially to determine whether all claimants are in receipt of universal credit, or whether there are existing legacy claims in place.

2.1 Part One – Universal Credit in place

2.1.1 Introduction

The aim of universal credit is to replace the complexity of different means tested benefits with a single benefit for people of working age. This will mean the disappearance of income support, income based job-seekers allowance, income related employment and support allowance, housing benefit, child tax credit and working tax credit.

For people who have reached pension age, the rules outlined in Part Two of this chapter will normally apply and universal credit will be irrelevant.

For those of working age, a person claiming universal credit will come under the universal credit system, and so will be subject to the rules in this part. This also applies to a person making a claim for employment and support allowance (formerly sickness and invalidity benefits) (contributory or means tested) or for jobseekers allowance (contributory or means tested). Generally, therefore, a new claimant will be paid universal credit, whereas an existing claimant may be paid either benefit, depending on the point which the phasing in of universal credit had reached when they made their claim. With effect from November 2020 (a date which however may well slip) existing claimants of the five legacy benefits and of tax credits will start to be transferred across to the new benefit.

It should be emphasised that the differences between old and new systems are in many cases not great, but there are certain variations which it helps to understand when advising on the way forward for a personal injury victim.

2.1.2 Entitlement to Universal Credit

A claimant must satisfy both the "basic conditions" and the "financial conditions". The basic conditions are:-

- The claimant must be 18 or over (some 16/17 year olds can qualify);

- The claimant must be below pension age;(see Appendix 1)
- The claimant must not be in education (again, there are some exceptions);
- The claimant must satisfy both the "right to reside" test and the "habitual residence" test, and must not be a person subject to immigration control;
- The clamant must have accepted a "claimant commitment" (which means a commitment to take whatever steps are relevant in his or her case to find work).

The financial conditions are:-

- The claimant's income is not too high;
- The claimant has capital of £16,000 or below.

The distinction between those who are working for more than 16 hours a week and those who are not becomes irrelevant in universal credit.

In the case of a couple, both must usually meet the qualifying conditions, and make a joint claim. In the case of a couple one of whom is below pension age and one of whom is above that age, it is the age of the younger that determines benefit entitlement, i.e. they will be entitled to universal credit, not to pension credit. It follows that a single person over pension age , or a member of a couple both of whom are over pension age, will have access to the more generous rules enshrined in the pension credit rules (whether pension credit has been introduced in their area or not), whereas a member of a couple whose partner is below pension age will be entitled to universal credit, with the accompanying less generous rules regarding personal injury compensation.

2.1.3 The capital rule in universal credit

Universal credit is calculated on a monthly, not a weekly, basis. If the claimant (together with his or her partner, if any) has more than £16,000 capital, they cannot claim universal credit. (Note that this may affect someone who was previously receiving tax credits, where the capital rule is different – see 2.2.11 below). If the claimant (and partner, if appropriate) has more than £6,000, but £16,000 or less, they are treated as receiving an income from the capital of £4.35 a month for every £250, or part of £250, above £6000. This is usually referred to as "tariff income".

There are several differences between the definition of capital within the old system (the legacy benefits) and universal credit, but in large measure the new system follows the old. Again the term 'capital' is not defined; generally, it includes savings, property, and payments such as statutory redundancy payment or personal injury compensation. Certain items are disregarded; the value of the home is ignored while the claimant is living in it, or during one of several specified temporary absences. Personal belongings are disregarded. There are some differences; for example, a payment to or for a child in need under section 17 of the Children Act 1989 is disregarded altogether under the legacy benefits, but is disregarded for twelve months only under universal credit. The value of a funeral plan contract is ignored indefinitely for universal credit but not for the legacy benefits.

The regulations covering universal credit are the **Universal Credit Regulations 2013 No 376.** Full details of capital which is to be disregarded are found in Schedule 10.

2.2 Part Two – Universal Credit not yet fully in place

2.2.1 Means Tested Benefits and tax credits

There are five means tested, or income based, benefits. These are:-

- Income support
- Income based jobseekers allowance
- Income related employment and support allowance
- Pension credit
- Housing benefit

Council tax benefit has now been replaced by local schemes.

There are two tax credits:-

- Child tax credit
- Working tax credit

All five means tested benefits, to a greater or lesser extent, take account both of capital resources and of income. All five are calculated by reference both to the resources of the claimant, and also to the resources of the claimant's partner (if any), whether married or not. It is important to note that the requirements and resources of a couple will be aggregated; if for example one member of a couple receives compensation for a personal injury, the benefit system will treat the money received as the capital of both of them.

Tax credits are operated by HMRC, and the qualifying conditions, and the calculations, are very different to the means tested benefits. However, it is convenient to deal with them in this section. They are dealt with at 2.2.8 below.

If there are dependent children, then in most (but not all) cases their support will be provided through the medium of tax credits rather than any of the means tested benefits listed above.

In addition to means tested benefits and tax credits, there are two other situations where a person's income and capital are relevant to their entitlements. These are where a local authority, acting under its community care duties, provides services to the individual in their home for which it is able to charge; and where a person is placed in residential care and where it is anticipated that all or part of the care home fees will be met by the local authority. In both such cases, a means test will determine entitlement to funding. These issues are dealt with in later chapters, although there is some similarity between them and the benefit system described here.

There are restrictions on means tested benefits for persons from abroad. Generally a claimant must satisfy both the "right to reside" test and the "habitual residence" test, and must not be a person subject to immigration control. A person defined as subject to immigration control by **section 115 of the Immigration and Asylum Act** 1999 is generally not entitled to any of the means tested benefits outlined here, but there are exceptions. This is a complex area, and specialist advice should be sought.

2.2.2 The Means Tested Benefits

Housing benefit is intended to provide assistance with rent. The other four benefits are intended to provide day to day living expenses. For a person over pension age, the appropriate benefit is usually pension credit. Someone of working age who is unable to work because of sickness or disability, and whose income is insufficient to meet their requirements, may be entitled to income related employment and support allowance; this benefit has replaced incapacity benefit. A person who is not so entitled will instead be entitled to income support if he or she is in a 'prescribed category'. A list of the main prescribed categories appears below.

The default benefit is income based jobseekers allowance. Anyone under pension age who is not entitled to either income support or income related employment and support allowance, or who is under pension age and not entitled to pension credit, will have to sign on as available for work as a condition of receiving the benefit, and will have to demonstrate that they are actively seeking work.

2.2.3 Income support

The main prescribed categories for income support are as follows:-

- A lone parent (including a foster parent) with child under 5;

- A person looking after a child aged under 16 for someone else;
- A carer who fulfils certain criteria;
- A pregnant woman who is incapable of work, or who is within the last eleven weeks of pregnancy;
- A refugee learning English;
- Certain young persons (16-18) in relevant education (i.e. up to A level) who do not have a parent to claim for them

Note that this is not an exhaustive list.

In order to qualify for income support, a person's income must be less than his or her 'applicable amount'. Applicable amounts are calculated by reference firstly to a personal allowance (single or couple) and secondly to 'premiums' for additional living costs occasioned by particular circumstances, largely consisting of either disability or caring responsibilities. For example, a couple, one of whom is disabled (as defined by the regulations), would have an applicable amount calculated (on 2020/21 rates) as follows:-

Personal allowance (couple both over 18)	£116.80
Premium for one disabled person	£49.80
Applicable amount	£166.60

Note that this calculation is intended for illustration only; this book does not seek to address the considerable complexities of benefit calculations. The interested reader is referred to the Child Poverty Action Group Handbook, details of which can be found in Chapter 11.

There is no longer (since 6 April 2018) any provision within the income support system for the payment of mortgage interest for a home owner. Instead, certain home owners may request a loan from the DWP to help with mortgage costs. This scheme, known as Support for Mortgage Interest, is outlined at https://www.gov.uk/support-for-mortgage-interest. A claimant may still receive help from the benefit system with certain housing costs which they are obliged to pay, such as service charges and ground rent.

Against the total applicable amount figure is set the income of the individual or couple. Not all income counts. Income support then pays the difference between the applicable amount and the income.

Most benefits count as income, but (importantly) personal independence payment and attendance allowance do not. This income is 'disregarded'. Most adult claimants of disability living allowance have now been transferred to personal independence payment, but any who have not yet been transferred will also have their disability living allowance disregarded.

The detailed operation of income support is found in the **Income Support (General) Regulations 1987 No 1967** (referred to in this work as "IS Regs"). Schedule 8 to those regulations set out the complex rules regarding income which is wholly or partly disregarded, and Schedule 9 sets out the equivalent rules for income other than earnings. All income not specifically disregarded is taken into account in full.

2.2.4 Income based jobseekers allowance

This is calculated in the same way as income support. The position with housing costs is the same as for income support. Instead of qualification being based on prescribed categories, however, there is a single qualifying condition, which is that the person is 'available for and actively seeking work'. Income based JSA is not to be confused with contributory JSA, which is payable on the basis of the individual's national insurance contributions for six months, and is not means tested.

The 'available for and actively seeking work' test is a contentious one. In order to qualify for JSA, a claimant must be available for and actively seeking work. This means being willing and able to take up work immediately; being available on any day of the week, and at any time of day; and being prepared to take a job that would involve at least 40 hours' work a week, but also being also willing to work part-time if this is offered. Clearly someone who is ill or disabled and unable to work is not caught by these rules, although the boundary is one which is not always easy to determine; a person whose claim for employment and support allowance (see next section) is refused will by default need to claim JSA and fulfil all the requirements of a successful claim. A series of sanctions enforce the rule; a person who is deemed not to be doing enough can have their benefit suspended.

Where the claimant is one of a couple, and neither is responsible for a child, the couple will have to make a joint claim for JSA.

In most cases, a new claim by a person seeking work will be a claim for universal credit rather than for JSA.

The relevant regulations ("JSA Regs") are the **Jobseeker's Allowance Regulations 1996 No 207.**

2.2.5 Income related employment and support allowance

A person who is sick and can produce sick notes from their doctor, and who is not entitled to statutory sick pay, can claim employment and support allowance (ESA). For the first 13 weeks of a claim they are in an 'assessment phase' and are paid benefit at the basic rate for a single person (£74.35 for someone over 25, at 2020/21 rates). During the assessment phase they will undergo certain tests to determine, firstly whether they have 'limited capability for work' (i.e. are entitled to go on receiving the benefit) and secondly, assuming they are, whether they also have 'limited capability for work related activity'. If they do have limited capability for work related activity, they are deemed to be in the 'support group'; their benefit increases at the end of the 13 week assessment phase by £39.20 with no further conditions. If they are not within this category, then they will receive a further £29.55 from week 14, on condition that they work with an adviser within the DWP to try to get them back to work. A failure to participate will result in sanctions, which will eventually reduce the basic benefit back to £74.35 a week.

The basis on which a person is deemed to have limited capability for work, or to have limited capability for work related activity, is by means of an award of points. The system, and the qualifying conditions, are described in Appendix 2.

ESA is a contributory benefit, and as such is not means tested. Anyone with the necessary contributions who fulfils the criteria is entitled to benefit, for a maximum of 365 days. However, for those with no or limited other sources of income, who are unable to meet their everyday living expenses, there is an income-based 'top-up' to ESA. It is calculated in a similar (but not identical) way to income support and income based jobseekers' allowance, including the same rules as to help with housing costs. It is the income based component to which the personal injury trusts rules apply. Like Contributory Jobseekers Allowance, contributory ESA is unaffected by capital, and therefore by any award of personal injury compensation.

The Regulations are the **Employment and Support Allowance Regulations 2008 No 794** ("the ESA Regs") which cover both contributory and means tested ESA.

2.2.6 Pension Credit

Pension credit is in two parts. The first part is called guarantee credit, and the second savings credit. Guarantee credit is similar to the other means tested benefits, in that it compares an actual income (once disregarded income has been taken out of the equation) with a hypothetical amount which the claimant is supposed to need If income is less than the applicable amount, pension credit pays the balance. Guarantee credit replaced income support or its equivalents for those who have reached pension age (see Appendix 1), and the main qualifying condition is that the claimant has attained that age. In the case of a couple, the benefit is payable when the younger of the couple reaches that age. As with other means tested benefits, obligatory service charges or ground rent can be included in the amount payable, but there is no longer any support for mortgage interest.

Savings credit is intended to reward those who have either savings or pension entitlement additional to the state pension (or both). Savings credit is being phased out from April 2016, and is not further considered here.

Details can be found in the **State Pension Credit Regulations 2002 No 1792** ("the PC Regs").

2.2.7 Housing Benefit

This works in a similar way to the benefits described above, in comparing income with applicable amount. The principal difference in the calculation is the addition of a third element, namely the amount of rent actually paid. The means test is used to determine whether the amount of benefit paid is the maximum (i.e. the amount of rent actually paid) or some lesser amount, either because the claimant has a higher income, or because he or she is deemed to be paying an excessive amount in rent.

A person who receives income support, income based jobseekers allowance, income related employment and support allowance, or guarantee credit, is 'passported' on to the highest amount of housing benefit that s/he is entitled to; because of restrictions on the amount of rent that will be met by benefit, it may be less than the rent actually paid – the 'eligible rent'.

There are separate regulations for those who have reached pension age and those who have not. The regulations are:-

- the **Housing Benefit Regulations 2006 No 213** ("HB Regs");
- the **Housing Benefit (Persons who have attained the Qualifying Age for State Pension Credit) Regulations 2006 No 214** ("HB (PC) Regs");

One of the effects of the Welfare Reform Act 2012 is that council tax benefit disappeared as a national benefit, and local authorities now operate their own schemes. These schemes may well operate a similar rule regarding capital; it is worth checking with your local authority to find out how they do deal with claims for council tax reduction.

2.2.8 Tax credits

There are two types of tax credit: working tax credit, and child tax credit. Child tax credit (CTC) is paid to families with children or dependent young people up to 18. It is non-contributory but means tested. It is paid irrespective of whether the claimant is working. It is payable to families whose main source of income is income support, income based jobseekers allowance, income related employment and support allowance, or the guarantee credit element of pension credit. It is also payable in its own right to those on low income. These benefits do not make provision for children.

Under the **Welfare Reform and Work Act 2016**, CTC is generally restricted to two children, and no provision is made for a child born on or after 6th April 2017.

Working Tax Credit (WTC) is payable to some low paid workers as a top-up to low pay. It is non-contributory but is means tested. In order to qualify a claimant or their partner must be in full-time work. This means working at least 30 hours a week, or 16 hours if the worker is disabled, or 60 or over, a single parent, or a couple with at least one child whose partner is incapacitated, or receives carers allowance, or is in hospital or prison.

In due course, existing tax credit claimants will be transferred to Universal Credit.

Tax credits are operated by HMRC and not by the DWP, and operate according to significantly different rules. In particular, they are calculated by reference to taxable income during the last complete tax year. In addition, the rules regarding capital are different. Details of the calculations are not set out here. However, it is important to note firstly that tax credits will in due course be subsumed into universal credit; and secondly that both benefits may be affected by income and capital received.

The Regulations are as follows:-

- **Child Tax Credits Regulations 2002 (SI No 2007/2002)**
- **Working Tax Credits (Entitlement and Maximum Rate) Regulations 2002 (SI No 2005/2002)**

2.2.9 Means tested benefits and capital

This section covers only the five means tested benefits. Capital and tax credits are considered at section 2.2.11 below.

Capital is not defined in any of the means tested benefit regulations. It is normally considered to include all assets which are not specifically 'disregarded', apart from personal possessions.

Schedule 10 of the **IS Regs** (with equivalent provisions for other benefits) provides for specified items of capital to be ignored (disregarded).

Capital of a partner is aggregated with the capital of the claimant for all means tested benefits. Capital of a child is normally ignored, unless the family is claiming income support for a child – from 2004 new claims for support for children have been met by the award of child tax credit, with existing income support claimants to be moved across to tax credits over time. This process, however, took significantly longer than expected, and any who continue to receive income support have a more restrictive rule on children's capital. With this exception, therefore, it follows that where personal injury compensation is awarded to a child, the benefits of the parents are unaffected – althuogh there may be other reasons (such as tax efficiency) which would make a personal injury trust appropriate.

2.2.10 The capital rule

All the five means tested benefits operate with a capital rule. There are two levels; the lower and higher level. For income support, income-based JSA, income related employment and support allowance, and housing benefit, the lower level is £6,000. The higher level is £16,000.

This means that a person with capital in excess of £16,000 will be disqualified for these benefits altogether. For everyone else, capital is disregarded entirely up to the lower level, but is thereafter taken into account in calculating income. The actual income received from the capital is ignored; instead there is a 'tariff' or deemed income calculation, which decrees that a person is deemed to receive £1 per week for every £250, or part of £250, which they hold which is above the lower level. A person with capital of £8,000, therefore, has a 'tariff income' of £8 per week, and a person with capital of £14,000 has a tariff income of £24 per week. The amount of tariff income is added to other income in calculating the final amount of benefit.

The lower capital level for pension credit is £10,000. Pension credit has no upper capital limit, so that there is (at least notionally) no limit on the capital a person can hold and still be entitled to pension credit (although in practice the tariff income would erode away any entitlement, e.g. a person with capital of £30,000 has a deemed or tariff income of £40 per week). The tariff income figure for pension credit is £1 for every £500 above the lower limit. The **Welfare Reform Act 2012 section 75** includes a power (not yet exercised) to impose an upper capital limit for pension credit.

The absence of an upper level applies also to those over pension credit age in respect of housing benefit. The only exception is that a person receiving savings credit but not guarantee credit, who also claims housing benefit, has an upper limit of £16,000 relating to housing benefit, although not to savings credit. A person receiving guarantee credit has a lower level of £10,000 for housing benefit.

Capital is not defined as such by any of the regulations. By common consent, capital includes money, in any form, and assets other than personal belongings. The value of a house (after deduction of any charges on it) counts as capital unless it can be disregarded under any of the Schedule 10 provisions in the case of income support, or the equivalents for the other benefits (for example, because the claimant lives in it, or is temporarily absent, or it is occupied by the claimant's spouse or an elderly or incapacitated relative). The capital which is included in the calculation of benefit is the capital of both the claimant and his or her partner.

It will be seen that the receipt of additional capital or income will therefore affect a person's entitlement to any of the above benefits. This is considered below as regards money paid in compensation for personal injury.

2.2.11 Tax credits and capital

Tax credits do not operate a capital rule in the same way as for the means tested benefits. For the purposes of tax credits, capital is ignored. However, unlike the tariff income arrangements for the means tested benefits, actual taxable income from savings and investments is taken into account, apart from the first £300 in a tax year.

It will therefore be appreciated that the detailed consideration of the deprivation of capital rules in Chapter 4 will not apply to tax credits.

CHAPTER THREE
HOW PERSONAL INJURY COMPENSATION IS DEALT WITH

3.1 Receipt of capital

Where a claimant receives a sum of money, it may be treated for benefits purposes as income or capital. On the whole, the difference should be apparent, although there are circumstances specified in regulations where money which appears to be income will be treated as capital or vice versa (for example, a lump sum settlement of a claim for underpaid wages under the **Equality Act 2010** is treated as income). Claimants are obliged to report promptly any change in their circumstances. A claimant who receives a legacy, for example, or who has a lottery win, is therefore obliged to notify the Department for Work and Pensions, who will recalculate benefit on the basis of the additional income or capital received. Note that the receipt of capital includes money which would be available to the claimant on applying for it, such as money in the hands of their solicitor (**Thomas v Chief Adjudication Officer, R(SB) 17/87)**. Note also that if the capital is disregarded, its receipt will make no difference to the amount of benefit. This is also the case when disregarded capital is converted into another form of disregarded capital. A receipt of disregarded capital, however, should be reported to the DWP even if it is known that it will be disregarded.

Where a claimant receives a payment of capital, there is therefore an obvious temptation to conceal it, or to seek to give it away, in order to retain benefits. This is likely to fall foul of the rule on the deprivation of capital.

3.2 Deprivation of capital

A person who deprives him or herself of capital, or who fails to take up capital to which he or she may be entitled, is liable to be treated by the benefits authorities as if they actually possessed that capital. This means, for example, that a person who gives away capital (which would otherwise have left them with capital in excess of the upper limit) as a gift, in order to reduce their declared capital below the upper limit, is likely to be denied benefit on the basis that they are deemed still to possess it. This is usually referred to as notional capital. If benefit is paid on the basis that a person has no capital above the upper limit, and it then becomes apparent that they did, there will have been an overpayment of benefit, which is then recoverable; this is common practice, for example, in the case of a deceased estate, when a grant of probate or letters of administration discloses a substantial undisclosed capital sum standing to the credit of the deceased on death.

It is therefore important to ensure that capital is assessed so that capital which does not count can be ignored, while capital that does count is declared promptly in order to avoid a bill later.

The procedure can be illustrated by an example. Suppose that George, who is in receipt of income based jobseekers allowance and housing benefit, and who has no capital, receives a legacy of £20,000 from the estate of a relative. If he declares it, he will be disqualified for both benefits, and will need to claim again once the capital is reduced (or is deemed to be reduced) below the upper limit. If he does not declare it, there will be an overpayment of benefit which will be recoverable from him. In calculating this, it will be assumed that his capital reduces at a set rate, and once it reduces below the upper limit, he will once more be entitled to benefit. This is so whether he had retained the money or given it away.

3.3 The personal Injury capital disregard – people under pension age

Originally, a payment of capital as compensation for personal injury was simply counted as part of the claimant's capital in the same way as any other receipt of capital, e.g. a legacy. This has been amended in two stages. Initially, changes introduced in 1998 provided that personal injury compensation would be disregarded if it was placed in a trust. This needed to be done quickly, as the compensation would count as the claimant's capital throughout the time after it was received but before it was placed in trust. This included where it was in the hands of the claimant's solicitor (**Thomas v Chief Adjudication Officer,** supra). In 2008, therefore, the rule was further amended to provide for a general disregard of any compensation paid for a personal injury in certain circumstances.

"Personal Injury Compensation" has a wide meaning. It includes not only payments for accidental and criminal injuries, but also for disease and for any injury sustained as the result of a disease. It includes money held in Court. It also includes damages for negligence against a firm of solicitors who had failed to make a claim in time (**KQ v SSWP (IS) [2011] UKUT 102 (AAC)).**

This section considers firstly the rules regarding income support, which were the first to be enacted in point of time, in order to show how the present arrangement has come about. The universal credit rules are for practical purposes the same; they are considered further below. References in this section to income support therefore should be taken to include reference to all other means tested benefits. In the case of income support, the relevant provision is **paragraph 12** of **Schedule 10** to the **IS Regs**, as amended initially by the **Income Support (General) Amendment No 3 Regulations 1990, SI 1990 No 1776**, and subsequently by the **Social Security (Miscellaneous Amendments) (No. 4) Regulations 2006 No 2378.**

The relevant provisions, so far as income support is concerned, now read:-

> [There shall be disregarded …]
>
> "*12. Where the funds of a trust are derived from a payment made in consequence of any personal injury to the claimant or the claimant's partner, the value of the trust fund and the value of the right to receive any payment under that trust.*

The second amendment, from 2008, provides:-

> [there shall be disregarded …]
>
> *12A. (1) any payment made to the claimant or the claimant's partner in consequence of any personal injury to the claimant or, as the case may be, the claimant's partner.*

(2) But sub-paragraph (1) –

(a) applies only for the period of 52 weeks beginning with the day on which the claimant first receives any payment in consequence of that personal injury;

(b) does not apply to any subsequent payment made to him in consequence of that injury (whether it is made by the same person or another);

(c) ceases to apply to the payment or any part of the payment from the day on which the claimant no longer possesses it;

(d) does not apply to any payment from a trust where the funds of the trust are derived from a payment made in consequence of any personal injury to the claimant.

(3) for the purposes of paragraph (2)(c), the circumstances in which the claimant no longer possesses a payment or a part of it include where the claimant has used a payment or part of it to purchase an asset.

(4) references in sub-paragraphs (2) and (3) to the claimant are to be construed as including references to his partner (where applicable)."

The same rule applies to income based jobseekers allowance, income related employment and support allowance, and housing benefit (but not pension credit – see below), and also (as noted above) to universal credit. The equivalent references for the legacy benefits are **Schedule 8**

para 17A JSA Regs; Schedule 9 para 17 ESA Regs; and **Schedule 6 para 14A HB Regs**.

The first part of the disregard is therefore in place for up to 52 weeks, and covers any compensation in respect of personal injury. "Personal injury" is widely defined, as outlined above (see for example R(SB) 2/89). Because of the explicit provisions of this regulation, the rules on deprivation of capital do not apply, and a claimant placing personal injury compensation into trust (whenever this takes place) will not be caught by the notional capital rules.

The 52 week period begins on receipt of the payment (or first payment), and the amount of the disregard diminishes at the same rate as that at which the capital is spent. It seems clear from the wording that the disregard only applies to the first payment. A subsequent payment will not be subject to any disregard at all unless it is put in trust.

Only compensation received for a personal injury can benefit from the disregard. This means that any money from other sources which is paid into the trust cannot be disregarded and will go towards the claimant's capital limit. Personal injury money in the trust will not be tainted by this, but it is important to keep appropriate records in such a case.

Once the money paid is placed into a trust fund, then the 52 week disregard comes to an end and the second disregard (see **paragraph 12** of the **IS Regs**, above) comes into effect. The value of the trust fund is now ignored with no time limit.

Lump sum payments from the trust back to the claimant are not covered by the 52 week disregard (see **IS Regs para 12A(2)(d)**, and equivalent provisions for other benefits).

In the case of a personal injury to the claimant's partner, the 52 week disregard comes to an end on that person's death. So too does the disregard applying to the trust fund **(R(IS) 3/03)**.

If the compensation is in respect of a child, then since generally the capital and the income of a child does not belong to the claimant, it is disregarded for the purposes of the claimant's claim, except as indicated above in respect of claims for income support which have been subsisting since before 6th April 2004.

Note that there is no specific requirement as to how the trust fund shall be set up or administered. In particular it is not necessary that it be set up by deed.

3.4 Universal Credit

The effect of the Universal Credit regulations is to replicate the previous scheme. By **Reg 75** of the **UC Regs**:-

> ***Compensation for personal injury***
>
> ***75.***—*(1) This regulation applies where a sum has been awarded to a person, or has been agreed by or behalf of a person, in consequence of a personal injury to that person.*

(2) If, in accordance with an order of the court or an agreement, the person receives all or part of that sum by way of regular payments, those payments are to be disregarded in the calculation of the person's unearned income.

(3) If the sum has been used to purchase an annuity, payments under the annuity are to be disregarded in the calculation of the person's unearned income.

(4) If the sum is held in trust, any capital of the trust derived from that sum is to be disregarded in the calculation of the person's capital and any income from the trust is to be disregarded in the calculation of the person's unearned income.

(5) If the sum is administered by the court on behalf of the person or can only be disposed of by direction of the court, it is to be disregarded in the calculation of the person's capital and any regular payments from that amount are to be disregarded in the calculation of the person's unearned income.

(6) If the sum is not held in trust or has not been used to purchase an annuity or otherwise disposed of, but has been paid to the person within the past 12 months, that sum is to be disregarded in the calculation of the person's capital.

Despite the different structure, the overall effect would appear to be the same as for the legacy benefits.

3.5 Trust Funds Administered by Court

In a case where damages awarded for personal injury or, in the case of a child under 18, for the death of one or both parents are administered by or under the control of the court, both the capital value of the trust and the income from it is ignored:

- **Regulation 75 (5) UC Regs.**
- **Schedule 10 paragraphs 44 and 45 IS Regs;**
- **Schedule 8 paragraphs 42 and 43 JSA Regs;**
- **Schedule 9 paragraphs 43 and 44 ESA Regs; and**
- **Schedule 6 paragraphs 45 and 46 HB Regs.**

3.6 The personal Injury capital disregard – people over pension age

The position with Pension Credit recipients is different. The rules above regarding a 52 week disregard, and the placing of compensation in trust, do not apply to those over the qualifying age for pension credit, unless they are receiving income support, income based job seekers allowance or income related employment and support allowance, rather than pension credit. This may be the case, for example, where the claimant has a younger partner.

For pension credit claimants, therefore, a payment of personal injury compensation is completely ignored, whether it is paid into a trust or not. The tariff income rule does not apply, and no actual income from the trust is taken into account. (**Schedule 6 paragraph 16(1) SPC**

Regs). This same rule applies in the case of housing benefit to those over 60 (**Schedule 6 paragraph 17(1) HB (SPC) Regs**). The rule does not apply where the compensation is in respect of a person who is no longer a member of the family because they have died (**R (IS) 3/03**).

3.7 Income from a personal injury trust

Rules cover the position of payments from the trust fund, whether as a regular payment or as an occasional sum.

Certain payments are disregarded if made regularly. These include:-

- payments from a trust fund set up from personal injury compensation;
- payments from an annuity purchased under an agreement or a court order resulting from a personal injury, or from any money paid because of a personal injury, or
- payments received under an agreement or court order because of any personal injury

(Reg 75 (2) UC Regs; Schedule 9 paragraph 15(5a) IS Regs; Schedule 7 paragraph 15(5a) JSA Regs; Schedule 8 paragraph 16(3) ESA Regs; Schedule 5 paragraph 14 HB Regs.)

An irregular payment from a trust fund is generally treated as capital and ignored.

In **Malekout v Secretary of State for Work and Pensions [2010] EWCA Civ 162** (2 February 2010), the claimant had been a dentist. As a result of an injury suffered during his employment, he received monthly payments from the NHS pension scheme. He sought to argue that they should be disregarded as income under the 'personal injury' provisions. His claim was disallowed by both the tribunal and the Deputy Commissioner, and he appealed to the Court of Appeal.

The relevant provision is to be found in **paragraph 15(1)** of **Schedule 9** to the **Income Support (General) Regulations 1987**. This provides that 'any relevant payment made or due to be made at regular intervals' is to be disregarded. A 'relevant payment' is defined as –

> *'(a) a charitable payment;*
>
> *(b) a voluntary payment;*
>
> *(c) a payment (not falling within sub-paragraph (a) or (b) above) from a trust whose funds are derived from a payment made in consequence of any personal injury to the claimant;*
>
> *(d) a payment under an annuity purchased (i) pursuant to any agreement or court order to make payments to claimant; or (ii) from funds derived from payment made, in consequence of any personal injury to the claimant; or*
>
> *(e) a payment (not falling within sub-paragraphs (a) to (d) above) received by virtue of any agreement or court order to make payments to the claimant in consequence of any personal injury to the claimant.'*

The claimant argued that his payments should be disregarded under paragraph (e) as being made under an agreement, namely his contract of employment with the NHS under which he was entitled to the pension for early retirement. However, the Court of Appeal disagreed. Sir David Keene said that the reasoning was as follows.

> *'The first is ... the preceding sub paragraphs. Those seem to me, particularly (c) and (d), to relate very much to the situation where the claimant has been injured and the consequential damages are put into a trust or used to purchase an annuity – a not uncommon occurrence. That suggests that sub-paragraph (e) is there in order to deal with the situation where a similar payment is made, but not via a trust or an annuity. The second piece of context which matters is the phrase in which the word 'agreement' appears. It is 'agreement or court order'. That does not, to my mind, indicate an agreement predating the personal injury, but an agreement which is reached instead of a court order after the injury has occurred. The contract of employment does not seem to be the sort of agreement indicated by that phrase.'* (paragraph 9)

A unanimous Court of Appeal dismissed the claimant's appeal.

CHAPTER FOUR
NON CONTRIBUTORY DISABILITY BENEFITS

These benefits are intended to meet the extra cost of disability. None of them is means tested, so the question of capital or of a personal injury trust does not affect their receipt, but in certain cases they provide a qualification for the means tested benefits. Details are included here for completeness, and to encourage advisors to inform clients what benefits might be available to them.

4.1 Personal Independence Payment

The Welfare Reform Act 2012 replaced disability living allowance (DLA) with a new benefit, known as Personal Independence Payment. The Act does not affect attendance allowance. Where the disabled person is a child under 16, they will still be able to claim disability living allowance.

The benefit (like DLA) must be claimed before the claimant reaches pension age. If their claim is successful, they can continue to receive the benefit beyond that age; but they cannot claim it for the first time after they have reached pension age.

The new scheme began to be introduced for adults from age 16 to age 64 with effect from April 2013 as a pilot, and was extended to the whole country from 10 June 2013. Those people receiving DLA at that date continued to be entitled to it, but virtually all such claimants have now been reassessed, and have either been transferred to PIP or have been disqualified. Reassessment does not apply, and they continue to receive DLA, if their 65th birthday (for a man or a woman) was on or before 8th April 2013.

A claimant must have met the conditions for at least three months and expect to continue to meet them for at least nine months, unless they are terminally ill (having a progressive disease from which death can reasonably be expected within six months).

The decision to award a payment or not will be taken by a decision maker, who will be advised by a 'trained independent assessor' who will gather information about the claimant, usually but not always including a face to face interview. Similarly to the work capability assessment for employment and support allowance, entitlement is based on a series of criteria, with points awarded for the extent to which the particular criterion is met. The two categories of criteria are 'daily living activities' and 'mobility activities'.

The qualifying conditions for the daily living activities are as follows:-

> *(1) A person is entitled to the daily living component at the standard rate if—*
>
> > *(a) the person's ability to carry out daily living activities is limited by the person's physical or mental condition;*
> >
> > ...
>
> *(2) A person is entitled to the daily living component at the enhanced rate if—*

(a) the person's ability to carry out daily living activities is severely limited by the person's physical or mental condition;

The qualifying conditions for the mobility activities are as follows:-

(1) A person is entitled to the mobility component at the standard rate if—

…

(b) the person's ability to carry out mobility activities is limited by the person's physical or mental condition;

…

(2) A person is entitled to the mobility component at the enhanced rate if—

…

(b) the person's ability to carry out mobility activities is severely limited by the person's physical or mental condition.

The daily living activities are:-

- Preparing food
- Taking nutrition
- Managing therapy or monitoring a health condition
- Washing and bathing
- Managing toilet needs or incontinence
- Dressing and undressing
- Communicating verbally
- Reading and understanding signs, symbols and words

- Engaging with other people face to face
- Making budgeting decisions

The mobility activities are:-

- Planning and following journeys
- Moving around

Entitlement is assessed by reference to a chart which allocates a number of points to a claimant. Where a claimant gets eight points or more ('limited'), they are entitled to the standard rate; where they get twelve points or more ('severely limited'), they are entitled to the enhanced rate. An example of the points scoring system is shown below. The full system is at Appendix 2.

1. Daily Living Activities	
Preparing food	**Pts**
a. Can prepare and cook a simple meal unaided	0
b. Needs to use an aid or appliance to be able to either prepare or cook a simple meal	2
c. Cannot cook a simple meal using a conventional cooker but is able to do so using a microwave	2
d. Needs prompting to be able to either prepare or cook a simple meal	2
e. Needs supervision or assistance to either prepare or cook a simple meal	4
f. Cannot prepare and cook food	8

4.2 Disability Living Allowance

This is a benefit for the extra cost of disability. It does not overlap with other benefits, and does not usually count as income for means tested benefits.

As noted above, it is now only payable to those who claimed it before 10 June 2013, who have not been reassessed for PIP; and to those under the age of 16, to whom PIP does not apply.

It is payable to those who claimed before pension age (with a possible extension beyond that age if the conditions continue to be met) in five possible sets of circumstances. The three care components are mutually exclusive, as are the two mobility components.

the **higher care component** is payable where the claimant needs attention or supervision **both** by day **and** at night;

the **middle care component** is payable where the claimant needs attention or supervision **either** by day **or** at night;

the **lower care component** is payable where the claimant needs help with bodily functions for a significant portion of the (24-hour) day, or help with preparing a cooked meal.

the **higher mobility component** is payable where because of a physical disability the claimant is unable or virtually unable to walk; or where because of a combination of blindness and deafness the claimant is unable to walk out of doors without help from another person; or where the claimant is unable to walk because of severe behavioural problems which qualify for the higher rate care component;

the **lower mobility component** is payable where the claimant can walk, but needs help and guidance in getting around.

The **day conditions** are that a person needs:

- frequent attention throughout the day in connection with their bodily functions; or
- continual supervision throughout the day to avoid substantial danger to themselves or others.

The **night conditions** are that a person needs:

- prolonged or repeated attention at night in connection with their bodily functions; or
- someone awake for a prolonged period or at frequent intervals for the purpose of watching over them.

The claimant must have needed this help for at least three months (unless they are terminally ill, in which case see below) and must expect to remain in that same condition for a further six months.

Care must be provided in the presence of the disabled person.

Someone who is terminally ill (defined as suffering from a progressive disease where death is reasonably to be expected within six months) receives the higher rate care component for life without a qualifying period.

Someone under 16 must require substantially more help than the average child of the same age in normal physical and mental health. A child can be awarded the care component from birth, but may not be awarded the higher mobility component until the age of 3, and the lower mobility component until the age of 5. On reaching 16, the child will be transferred from disability living allowance to PIP.

A claimant must claim before they reach pension age, but benefit can be awarded to continue beyond that age. A person who turned 65 before 10 April 2013 is unaffected by PIP unless their condition changes. If it does not, they can renew an existing award of DLA even after they have reached 65, provided they do so within one year, and in certain circumstances may become entitled to an additional or replacement component.

A person who was under 65 on 10 April 2013 will be invited, on termination of an existing DLA award, to claim for PIP instead.

4.3 Attendance Allowance

Attendance allowance is the equivalent of disability living allowance (see above) for those aged over pension age.

It is payable to someone who is over pension age when they first claim, and who is so disabled as to fulfil the conditions for either the higher or the lower rate. These are the same as the higher and middle rate care component of DLA, as set out above. Those needing help by day and at night receive the higher rate; those needing help either by day or at night receive the lower. A person aged over pension age when they first claim cannot claim for either of the mobility components, or for any equivalent of the DLA lower rate care component.

The qualifying period is six months (not three) unless the claimant is terminally ill. The special rules for terminally ill people apply in the same way as they do for DLA.

4.4 Industrial Disablement Benefit

Where the claimant has suffered personal injury as the result of an accident at work, or is suffering from a prescribed disease, they will be entitled to employment and support allowance without having to show that they have the contribution conditions.

They may also be entitled to an industrial disablement pension. The claimant must be in employed earners employment. They must have suffered personal injury by accident arising out of and in the course of their employment.

Someone who is assessed as at least 20% disabled is entitled to a weekly pension of £36.40, rising to £182.00 for a person who is 100% disabled (2020/21 rates).

Someone who is assessed as 100% disabled may be entitled to constant attendance allowance. If the disability is expected to be permanent, they may also be entitled to exceptionally severe disablement allowances. These additions are more generous than disability living allowance or attendance allowance.

Constant attendance allowance is paid at two main rates, the lower rate (where someone is to a substantial extent dependent on constant attendance for the necessities of life and is likely to remain so dependent for a prolonged period) which is £72.80 a week, and the higher rate, where someone is so severely disabled as to be entirely, or almost entirely, dependent on constant attendance for the necessities of life, and is likely to remain so dependent for a prolonged period, and the attendance so required is whole-time. The higher rate is £145.60 a week. The lower rate can be increased to a middle rate of £109.20 where the need is greater owing to exceptionally severe disablement. There is a lower rate of £36.40 a week (officially "such sum as may be reasonable") where the need for attendance is part-time.

Exceptionally severe disablement allowance is an additional £72.80 where the claimant gets CAA at least at the rate of £109.20 a week, and the need for attendance is likely to be permanent. (All rates are 2020/21.)

CHAPTER FIVE
LOCAL AUTHORITY SERVICES

Under Section 9 of the Care Act 2014, local authorities in England are legally obliged to assess anyone who comes to their notice as being potentially in need of care and support due to a physical or mental impairment. This is the case irrespective of whether the authority thinks it is likely that the person will or will not qualify for any care and support, and also irrespective of the person's financial situation (section 9(3)(b)).

In Wales, the legal position, although similar, is legislated differently. The powers and duties of local authorities are included in the **Social Services and Well-being (Wales) Act 2014**, which came into force on 1st April 2016. The Welsh provisions are considered separately below. It is important to note that, whereas the English provisions consider only adults, the Welsh provisions also cover children, and with that in mind, **Part 3** of the **Children Act 1989** has been largely repealed in Wales, and re-legislated within the **Social Services and Well-Being (Wales) Act.**

In both jurisdictions, the duty of a local authority is not just owed to those who need care and support, but also their carers.

As well as the two principal statutes, there are regulations in both countries which expand on the duties and responsibilities under the Acts. In England there is Statutory Guidance which at present is only in a digital form; it can be accessed at https://www.gov.uk/government/publications/care-act-statutory-guidance/care-and-support-statutory-guidance and is updated from time to time, most recently on 2nd March 2020.

In Wales there is a Code of Practice which can be accessed at http://gov.wales/topics/health/socialcare/act/code-of-practice/?lang=en

The appropriate document should be consulted for detailed information regarding the system which is now in operation.

5.1 Qualifying for care and support: England

5.1.1 The Single Assessment

An **assessment** is the process of considering a person's circumstances and making a decision about whether they need care and support to help them live their day-to-day lives. The assessment for care and support is usually carried out by a social worker, and will consider the presenting needs as well as the person's other circumstances. The assessment:

- must be of the adult's needs and the outcomes they want to achieve;
- must be provided to all people who appear to have some need for care and support, and therefore should not consider unrelated factors such as a person's finances;

- must not consider whether the local authority thinks the person will be eligible for services (see **R v Bristol CC ex parte Penfold (1998) 1 CCLR 315**); and
- must be carried out with involvement from the adult and, where appropriate, their carer or someone else they nominate.

Unlike the community care legislation which the **Care Act** replaced, there is no categorisation of individuals according to type (so for example the definition of a disabled person, formerly in **section 29** of the **National Assistance Act 1948**, disappears). Nor is there a list of potential services. There is an illustrative (but expressly not exhaustive) list in section 8(1) of what **may** be provided to an adult or carer, including

- accommodation in a care home or other premises;
- care and support at home or in the community;
- counselling, advocacy and other types of social work;
- goods and facilities;
- information and advice.

The **Eligibility Regulations** (see below) make clear that the determination of an adult's eligible needs is made without taking into account any support which is being provided by a carer. "Instead, where a person receives support from a carer, this will be taken into account during the development of the care and support plan", according to a discussion document in 2013. The term used for this is "carer blind assessments". Note that this particular provision is one of those which differs significantly in Wales, as discussed below.

The duty to assess, as noted above, arises irrespective of the authority's preliminary determination of whether the person will qualify, and also irrespective of his or her financial position. **Section 9 (1)** says:-

> *Where it appears to a local authority that an adult may have needs for care and support, the authority must assess—*
>
> *(a) whether the adult does have needs for care and support, and*
>
> *(b) if the adult does, what those needs are.*

Note that the appearance of need is sufficient; and that there is no need for an application.

After conducting the needs assessment, the local authority is then required to determine whether the person has eligible needs, using a national eligibility framework which (unlike the former legislation) is now statutory.

5.1.2 Entitlement to Care and Support

An adult must satisfy three requirements:-

- their needs must be the result of a physical or mental impairment or illness;
- as a result they must be unable to achieve **two or more** specified outcomes; and

- as a consequence, there is (or is likely to be) a **significant** impact on their well-being.

A person is 'unable' to achieve an outcome if they:-

- are unable to achieve it without assistance;
- are able to achieve it without assistance but only where it causes them significant pain, distress or anxiety;
- or able to achieve it without assistance but doing so will endanger their health or safety, or that of others, or
- achieving it would take significantly longer than would normally be expected.

The outcomes are:-

- managing and maintaining nutrition;
- managing personal hygiene;
- managing toilet needs;
- being appropriately clothed;
- being able to make use of their home safely;
- maintaining a habitable home environment;
- developing and maintaining family or other personal relationships; accessing and engaging in work, training, education or volunteering;
- making use of necessary facilities or services in the local community including public transport; and

- carrying out caring responsibilities which the person has for a child.

(Care Act 2014, sec 13(7); Care and Support (Eligibility Criteria) Regulations 2015, SI 2015/313)

The term "physical or mental impairment" is not defined by the Act, but paragraph 6.105 of the Guidance says that this refers to "physical, mental, sensory, learning or cognitive disabilities or illnesses, substance misuse or brain injury." It is clear that this wide interpretation is intended to encompass such descriptions as "any disorder or disability of the mind" as in section 1 of the **Mental Health Act 1983.**

The eligibility criteria may be overridden in case of emergency, as with the old law.

5.1.3 Duty and power to provide care and support

This is covered by sections **18-20** of the **Act.** Where an individual's needs meet the criteria, there is a duty to ensure that their care and support needs are met, provided they are ordinarily resident in the local authority's area. If their capital or income exceeds the limits, there will nevertheless be a duty on the authority to meet those needs for care and support.

5.2 Qualifying for care and support: Wales

5.2.1 The Single Assessment

Section 19 of the **Social Services and Well-Being (Wales) Act 2014** imposes a duty on local authorities to carry out assessments in order to determine whether an adult has needs for care and support. It says

> *(1) Where it appears to a local authority that an adult may have needs for care and support, the authority must assess—*
>
> *(a) whether the adult does have needs for care and support, and*
>
> *(b) if the adult does, what those needs are.*

As in England, the appearance of need is sufficient to trigger the duty.

There are similar provisions for carers (not further covered in this work) and for children (see below). **Section 19** requires that the assessment:

- must be of the adult's needs and the outcomes they want to achieve;
- must be provided to all people who appear to have some need for care and support, and therefore should not consider unrelated factors such as a person's finances;
- must not consider whether the local authority thinks the person will be eligible for services (see **R v Bristol CC ex parte Penfold,** supra); and
- must be carried out with involvement from the adult and, where appropriate, their carer or someone else they nominate.

Unlike the previous legislation (which was the same in Wales as in England, apart from some differences in the regime for payment for and funding of services), there is no categorisation of individuals according to type, as mentioned above; however, the question of whether a child is or is not classified as disabled remains relevant to determining the rights of his or her carers. Happily the definition of disability in section 29 of the **National Assistance Act 1948**, which also appears in section 17 of the **Children Act 1989**, has disappeared in Wales, and the definition of disability is brought into line with that in the **Equality Act 2010**, subject to limiting regulations (although the old definition survives in England, in section **17(11)** of the **Children Act 1989**).

The assessment process is governed by the **Care and Support (Assessment) (Wales) Regulations 2015**. Part 3 of the Code of Practice specifies the minimum content of the record of the assessment. The Guidance states at para 63 that there should be a comprehensive analysis of five key elements:

- The person's circumstances;
- Their personal outcomes;
- The barriers to achieving those outcomes;
- The risks to them or to others if those outcomes are not achieved; and
- The person's strengths and capabilities.

Part 3 also makes clear (at para 80) that when undertaking an assessment the authority "must identify all presenting needs including those which would be deemed as eligible if a carer were not meeting those needs." As noted above, under the English regulations, the determination of an adult's eligible needs is made without taking into account any support which is being provided by a carer. In Wales, however, care provided by a willing carer is not ignored for eligibility purposes, but the information is intended to enable the authority to respond when the carer becomes unable or unwilling to continue to meet the needs.

As also noted above, as well as covering adults, the Welsh legislation covers children. **Sections 21 to 23** govern the assessment of children in need. This is an addition to the previous law, which dealt (in **section 17 Children Act 1989**) with children in need, but did not provide any explicit statutory duty to carry out an assessment. The duty is similar to that for an adult. The appearance of need is sufficient to trigger the duty.

Section 21 requires that the assessment:

- must be of the child's needs and the outcomes they want to achieve, and that those with parental responsibility for the child wish to achieve for him or her;
- must be provided to all children who appear to have some need for care and support, and therefore should not consider unrelated factors such as the child's finances, or the finances of those with parental responsibility for the child;
- must not consider whether the local authority thinks the person will be eligible for care and support, or support; and

- must be carried out with involvement from the child and anyone with parental responsibility for him or her.

Section 21(7) creates a presumption that a child who is disabled has needs for additional or substitute care and support. The same provisions as to the identification of needs which are being met by a carer apply to a child as to an adult.

5.2.2 Entitlement to Care and Support

After conducting the needs assessment, the local authority is then required to determine whether the person has eligible needs. If they do, then consideration moves to the provision of care and support to meet those needs. There is now a national standard for eligibility, governed by the **Care and Support (Eligibility) (Wales) Regulations 2015**

There are four stages, which generally speaking apply to all potential recipients of care or support – adults, children, and carers. The four stages are:-

- The need arises for a specified reason (care, disability, etc)
- The need relates to certain outcomes
- The person is unable to meet that need even with available support from others.
- The need cannot be met unless the local authority provides or arranges services, or makes direct payments.

1. The specified reasons are:-

- In the case of an adult in need (**reg 3**), the need arises from their physical or mental ill-health, age, disability, dependence on drugs or alcohol, or other similar circumstances;
- In the case of a child in need (**reg 4**), they have needs as for an adult (above) or if the needs are unmet, they are likely to have an adverse effect on the child's development;
- In the case of a carer (**reg 5**), the need arises as a result of providing care for an adult in need (as described above) or for a disabled child.

2. The need must relate to a set of standard tasks. These are:-

- Ability to carry out self-care or domestic routines
- Ability to communicate
- Protection from abuse or neglect
- Involvement in work, education, learning or leisure activities
- Maintenance or development of family or other significant personal relationships
- Development and maintenance of social relationships and involvement in the community.

"Basic self-care" is defined in regulation 1. It consists of:-

> "*Tasks that a person carries out as part of daily life including*
>
> - *Eating and drinking*
> - *Maintaining personal hygiene*

- *Getting up and getting dressed*
- *Moving around the home*
- *Preparing meals*
- *Keeping the home clean, safe and hygienic"*

In addition there are two specific eligible tasks for, respectively, adults and children. For an adult the task is to be able to fulfil their caring responsibilities for a child. For a child (or a child carer) the task is to achieve developmental goals.

3. The person (and his or her parents, if s/he is a child) is not able to meet that need, either-

- Alone, or
- With the help of others willing to provide support, or
- With the assistance of community services to which the person has access.

The effect is that, if a person is able to meet the need with the support of a carer, they are ineligible – as opposed to England where assessments are "carer blind".

4. The person is unlikely to achieve one or more of the personal outcomes unless the local authority provides or arranges for care and support to meet the need.

The responsibility for determining whether the person is eligible and whether generalised services have been tried and have failed is on the assessor. The Part 4 Code says:-

> *"32. The eligibility criteria must not be used as a tool to require individuals to demonstrate they have exhausted every other possible avenue of support before becoming eligible for local authority assistance.*
>
> *33. It is the responsibility of the local authority to identify and record … how the personal outcomes will be achieved."*

5.2.3 Duty and power to provide care and support

The requirement of the former legislation that an assessment determined whether there was a need for "services" has been repealed. The new legislation, in **section 34**, sets out an illustrative list of ways in which a local authority may meet needs, as follows.

> *The following are examples of the ways in which a local authority may meet needs under sections 35 to 45—*
>
> > *(a) by arranging for a person other than the authority to provide something;*
> >
> > *(b) by itself providing something;*
> >
> > *(c) by providing something, or by arranging for something to be provided, to a person other than the person with needs for care and support (or, in the case of a carer, support).*
>
> *(2) The following are examples of what may be provided or arranged to meet needs under sections 35 to 45—*

(a) accommodation in a care home, children's home or premises of some other type;

(b) care and support at home or in the community;

(c) services, goods and facilities;

(d) information and advice;

(e) counselling and advocacy;

(f) social work;

(g) payments (including direct payments);

(h) aids and adaptations;

(i) occupational therapy.

Where an individual's needs meet the criteria, there is a duty under **sections 35 to 45** to ensure that their care and support needs are met, provided they are ordinarily resident in the local authority's area. If their capital or income exceeds the limits, there will nevertheless be a duty on the authority to meet those needs for care and support.

As well as imposing this right, it also strengthens the position of a "child in need"; it converts the power to make provision for carers into a duty; and it adds a duty to meet the needs of those who, although they fail to meet the eligibility criteria, are considered to be at risk of abuse or neglect.

The primary responsibility is to those who are ordinarily resident in the local authority's area. There is power to meet the needs of those whose needs are insufficient to meet the eligibility criteria; and there is still a limitation on meeting the needs of those who are subject to immigration control.

5.2.4 Duty to meet the needs of adults

These are little different to the previous law, except that the duty is extended to self-funders. The relationship with needs being met by a carer (discussed above) is explicitly stated in **section 35(6)** – the duty to meet the needs of an otherwise eligible adult "does not apply … to the extent that the local authority is satisfied that those needs are being met by a carer."

5.2.5 Duty to meet the needs of children

Unlike the limited duty under the previous legislation, **section 37** makes explicit the duty to provide all children with the care and support they are assessed as needing, or to protect them from harm.

The duty under **sec 37** does not apply to children who are "looked after", for which the Act makes detailed provisions in Part 6 (**Sections 74-125**). The provisions for looked after children which are found in the English **Children Act 1989 (section 22**) have been superseded. In addition, the effect of the Welsh legislation is to remove the definition of a child in need from **section 17** of the **Children Act 1989** and replace it with the definitions of the new Act. Part 3 of the **Children Act 1989** now only applies to England.

The Act does not contain any provisions which deal with a disabled child or their carers when a young person is in transition to adulthood.

CHAPTER SIX
PAYING FOR CARE

Someone with needs arising from a personal injury may require help and support from the health services or with personal care. This may be available free of charge, or for payment, which in certain cases is means tested. This chapter considers how the health and care systems operate, how they are paid for, and the possible effect on the finances of the injured party of receipt of a sum of money by way of compensation.

The systems in England and Wales differ, though not in every respect. They are therefore considered separately.

Where the individual's needs are health care needs, they are the responsibility of the National Health Service, which operates on the principle of services being free at the point of use. This is considered further below in Chapter 7.

Where the needs are not considered to meet the test of continuing health care needs, they will be needs which may be covered as appropriate either by the **Care Act 2014** or by the **Social Services and Well-Being (Wales) Act 2014** and their subordinate legislation. The services will therefore require an assessment of whether the individual should meet the whole or part of the cost. This is determined by a means test. Certain individuals will receive services free of charge. Others will pay something towards their care, and still others will pay the whole cost.

The basic outline of the system of charging is the same in both countries. Some services are specifically designated as free of charge. Apart from these, there are two parts to the means test in both countries; similarly to the means tested benefits described above, there will be a capital test and an income test. As a general rule, if the individual possesses capital in excess of the upper capital limit, he or she will be expected to pay the whole cost of their (non-NHS) care, and their income is irrelevant. If they do not, then the income test will determine what if anything they must pay towards the costs.

It will therefore be noted at once that, for the purposes of this book, a personal injuries settlement which is in excess of the upper capital limit will in the same way as with the benefit system preclude access to paid local authority care, unless that sum can be disregarded.

In England (but not in Wales) there is also a lower capital limit. Capital below the lower limit is disregarded entirely. Capital which falls between the two figures is subject to an income test, which provides for a tariff income in a similar way as for social security benefits. This system is explained above in Chapter 3. In England, therefore, receipt of a capital sum which falls below the upper capital limit but above the lower capital limit attracts a tariff income which may reduce the amount payable for care by the local authority; this in turn can be avoided if the capital sum can be disregarded.

6.1 Paying for care: the English system

Certain items are free of charge. These are as follows.

- The provision of community equipment (aids and adaptations);

- Intermediate care and reablement services, for a period of six weeks;
- Services provided to a person suffering from variant Creutzfeldt-Jakob Disease;
- Any service which is the responsibility of the NHS, including continuing health care;
- Any service which the local authority is under a duty to meet under other legislation; and
- Assessment and care planning.

In addition, services provided under the **Mental Health Act 1983 section 117** may not be charged for **(R (Stennett) v Manchester City Council [2002] 2 AC 1127**). **Section 117** imposes a duty on the local authority and the local clinical commissioning group to provide after care services to anyone who has been discharged after being detained under a treatment section of the Mental Health Act.

The two capital limits in England are:-

- Upper capital limit: £23,250
- Lower capital limit: £14,250

The tariff income figure referred to above is £1 for every £250 above the lower limit, irrespective of age. Someone with capital of £14,250 will therefore contribute nothing from their capital towards the cost of their care. Someone with capital of between £14,250.01 and £14,500.00 will contribute £1 every week. Someone with capital of between £14,500.01 and £14,750 will pay £2, and so on.

Capital includes money in virtually any form. It will therefore include personal injury compensation. However, by virtue of **Care and Support (Charging and Assessment of Resources) Regulations 2014,** Schedule 2, there shall be disregarded:-

> "***15.*** *Any amount which would be disregarded under paragraph 12 of Schedule 10 to the Income Support Regulations (personal injury trusts).*
>
> ***16.*** *Any amount which would be disregarded under paragraph 12A of Schedule 10 to the Income Support Regulations (personal injury payments) with the exception of any payment or any part of any payment that has been specifically identified by a court to deal with the cost of providing care.* "

The statutory guidance, at Annex B paragraph 33, refers to the following being disregarded:-

> "*(h) the value of funds held in trust or administered by a court which derive from a payment for personal injury to the person. For example, the vaccine damage and criminal injuries compensation funds*
>
> ...
>
> *(j) capital derived from an award of damages for personal injury which is administered by a court or which can only be disposed of by a court order or direction*

(k) the value of the right to receive any income under an annuity purchased pursuant to any agreement or court order to make payments in consequence of personal injury or from funds derived from a payment in consequence of a personal injury and any surrender value of such an annuity

(l) periodic payments in consequence of personal injury pursuant to a court order or agreement to the extent that they are not a payment of income and area (sic) treated as income (and disregarded in the calculation of income)

The position in Wales is similar (see 6.2.7 below).

The question which is commonly considered most problematic in this area is the question of whether an individual who is assessed as needing some measure of care and support owns a house; if he or she does so, then the value of the house will count as the person's capital unless it can be disregarded. In England, under the **Care and Support (Charging and Assessment of Resources) Regs 2014, Schedule 2, para 6,** a house is disregarded in effect while the owner is living in it. It follows that, where care is provided in the person's own home, its value will be irrelevant to the question of how much should be paid for the care and support provided. The point at which this commonly becomes a vexed issue, however, is the point at which the individual enters a residential or nursing home on a permanent basis. It is likely to be necessary for the person then to pay the full cost of their care, unless the capital value of the house can be disregarded. Annex B to the Statutory Guidance provides that the value of the former home will be disregarded in the following circumstances:-

(a) where the person is receiving care in a setting that is not a care home

(b) if the person's stay in a care home is temporary and they either:

   i. intend to return to that property and that property is still available to them

   ii. are taking reasonable steps to dispose of the property in order to acquire another more suitable property to return to

(c) where the person no longer occupies the property but it is occupied in part or whole as their main or only home by any of the people listed below, the mandatory disregard only applies where the property has been continuously occupied since before the person went into a care home (for discretionary disregards see below):

   i. the persons partner, former partner or civil partner, except where they are estranged

   ii. a lone parent who is the person's estranged or divorced partner;

   iii. a relative as defined in paragraph 35 of the person or member of the person's family who is either:

      1. aged 60 or over

      2. is a child of the resident aged under 18

      3. is incapacitated

Because this book is concerned with capital which arises from a specific and separate source, this question has comparatively little relevance.

However, it may become an issue where personal injury compensation is invested in a house for the injured person to live in, where that person later becomes unable to support him or herself in their own home and is forced to enter care. Thought should be given to how this might be prevented at the point of acquisition, for example by considering whether the value of the house might be disregarded, for instance because it is occupied by a carer, or failing that whether appropriate arrangements might be made by the trust deed, bearing in mind the rules as to deprivation and the specific tax rules governing residential property.

The issue of disregarding personal injury compensation in determining whether a person should pay towards their care was considered in the case of **R (ZYN) v Walsall MBC [2014] PTSR 1356 (HC)**, which is dealt with in Chapter 9 below.

Income from the trust is similarly disregarded. **Schedule 1 to the Care and Support (Charging and Assessment) Regs** provides (in England) for the following to be disregarded:-

> ***15.***—*(1) Except where sub-paragraph (2) applies … any relevant payment made or due to be made at regular intervals …*
>
> *(2) … any relevant payment made or due to be made at regular intervals which is intended and used for any item which was not specified in the personal budget but was specified in the care and support plan or support plan.*
>
> *(3) In this paragraph, "relevant payment" means—*

…

(c) a payment (not falling within sub-paragraph (a) or (b)) from a trust whose funds are derived from a payment made in consequence of any personal injury to the adult;

(d) a payment under an annuity purchased—

(i) pursuant to any agreement or court order to make payments to the adult; or

(ii) from funds derived from a payment made,

in consequence of any personal injury to the adult; or

(e) a payment (not falling within sub-paragraphs (a) to (d)) received by virtue of any agreement or court order to make payments to the resident in consequence of any personal injury to the adult.

6.1.2 Paying for Domiciliary Services: England

Where a person is provided with domiciliary services which are funded by the local authority, the authority is entitled to make a charge if they so determine (**Care Act section 14**). Note that they do not have to do so. The charges are based on a national statutory scheme and are covered by the **Care and Support (Charging and Assessment of Resources) Regulations 2014.** Guidance is found in the Care and Support Statutory Guidance, particularly chapters 8 and 9, and annexes A to E.

The Guidance (at para 8.2) includes a set of principles for local authorities to take into account in determining charges, namely:-

- Ensure people are not charged more than it is reasonable for them to pay;
- Be comprehensive, to reduce variations;
- Be clear and transparent;
- Promote wellbeing and social inclusion, and "support the vision of" personalisation, independence, choice and control;
- Support carers to look after their own needs and to care effectively;
- Be person-focused;
- Apply the charging rules equally and minimise the differences and anomalies between individual care settings;
- Encourage people to take up, or to stay in, employment, education or training, or plan for the future costs of their doing so;
- Be sustainable for local authorities in the long term.

It had been intended to make changes to the system of paying for care which would, among other provisions, introduce a lifetime cap on the amount to be paid for care. That provision was in the **Care Act 2014** and was intended to be introduced from April 2016, but was initially postponed until April 2020. Since payment for social care remains a subject of political debate, these changes will not now take place as planned, and await further legislation.

The means test is similar to, but not identical to, the means tested schemes used for benefits. In particular it should be noted that the means of a resident are <u>not</u> aggregated with those of his or her partner, unlike the social security benefits position. (However, care should be taken if it is felt that a person can therefore dispose of all or part of his or her capital by giving it to their partner, as the rules on deprivation of capital referred to above will apply.)

Where a local authority places a person in residential accommodation, and that person lacks capacity, the local authority may not disclaim their liability to pay the fees on the basis that the resident has enough capital and income to be regarded as a self-funder; see **Aster Healthcare v the Estate of Mohammed Shafi [2014] EWCA Civ 1350.**

6.1.3 Couples and Financial assessments

Unlike the benefits system, the Care Act does not require the aggregation of the needs and resources of a couple. The consequence is that each person should be assessed according to their individual means. This may prove difficult if the financial resources of a couple are inextricably linked, and care should be taken to separate the two where one partner goes into a care home, in order that the capital of one partner should not be used to meet the care home costs of the other.

Where there is joint beneficial ownership of capital, the authority will normally divide the total value equally between them, but evidence may be adduced to show that the shares are in fact unequal.

Take the example of a couple, one of whom receives compensation for a personal injury, where the other goes into residential care. Can the compensation be used to pay for the care for the partner? The wording of the disregard is such that it covers personal injury to the recipient but not to his or her partner. If it is in trust, then it is submitted it can be disregarded entirely for the needs of the other partner; but even if it is not, it is still the capital of one party, and any attempt by a local authority to argue that it is joint capital (even if in a joint account) should be resisted, as it is clearly the capital of one member of the couple, namely the injured party.

In a case where the resident is receiving an occupational pension, a personal pension, or payment from a retirement annuity contract, and he or she has a spouse or civil partner who is not living in the same care home, 50% of that payment should be disregarded provided the resident passes 50% onto the spouse.

If the resident passes less than 50% to the spouse for any reason, the disregard does not apply and the whole amount becomes payable (see **Care and Support (Charging and Assessment of Resources) Regulations 2014, Schedule 1, para 16**).

In other cases where the financial contribution from the resident could lead to hardship for a partner remaining at home, the local authority has power to allow a different amount for personal expenses in special circumstances. The authority may wish to increase the resident's personal expenses allowance. However, this is an entirely discretionary procedure. As it is discretionary, then it is open to use this in the case of parties who are not spouses or not civil partners.

6.2 Paying for Care: Wales

6.2.1 Funding Regulations

It should be noted that the Welsh legislation covers both adults and children, whereas the English Care Act covers only adults. The care and support of children in England is generally a function of the Children Act 1989 as amended.

The statutory provisions are contained in Part 5 of the **Social Services and Well-Being (Wales) Act 2014.** Where a person is placed in residential accommodation or is provided with domiciliary services which are funded by the local authority, the authority is entitled to make a charge if they so determine (**section 59**). They are also empowered by **section 69** to charge for preventative services. Note that they do not have to do so. The charge may not exceed the cost to the authority of its costs of meeting the need.

If they do charge, then they must follow the regulations (**Care and Support (Charging) (Wales) Regulations 2015** (the "Charging Regulations") and the **Care and Support (Financial Assessment) (Wales) Regulations 2015** (the "Financial Assessment Regulations") both as amended), and also the provisions of Parts 4 and 5 of the Code of Practice (which takes the place of the Statutory Guidance in Wales). Version 4 of the Code of Practice on charging and financial assessment came into force in April 2019.

There are separate regimes for charging someone who is living in a residential setting, or at home or elsewhere in the community. However, there are a number of common features.

6.2.2 Needs Assessments and Financial Assessments

The normal approach to the means test is to consider only the circumstances of the individual involved, and not those of his or her spouse or partner. Regulations provide for the means test.

In the case of jointly owned income or capital, the starting presumption is that they hold it in equal shares (**Financial Assessment Reg 24**). The local authority can assess income or capital jointly, but only where this would be more advantageous to the person concerned.

6.2.3 People who lack capacity

A local authority must have policies as to how they communicate, how they carry out a financial assessment, and how they collect any charges from a person without capacity. They must consult with family members. Where possible, they should also work with someone with the legal status to make a decision; if there is no such person, then an application to the Court of Protection may be required (Code of Practice Parts 4 and 5, para 5.5).

6.2.4 Children

A local authority may not charge a child for care and support, or for support in the case of a young carer.

6.2.5 Capital Limit

There is a standard capital limit of £50,000. This applies both when determining charges for residential accommodation and for domiciliary care. A person with capital above the limit pays the whole cost of their care. A person with capital below the limit is paid for. There is no lower capital limit as in England. The rules as to deprivation continue to apply, and are discussed further below.

The case of **Aster Healthcare v the Estate of Mohammed Shafi [2014] EWCA Civ 1350** is of application in Wales as well as in England. Where a local authority places a person in residential accommodation, and that person lacks capacity, the local authority may not disclaim their liability to pay the fees on the basis that the resident has enough capital and income to be regarded as a self-funder.

6.2.6 Contribution for those below the capital limits – means test

Certain services must be provided free of charge. These include:-

- care and support provided as reablement arranged under Part 2 (General functions) or Part 4 (Meeting needs) of the Act, or reablement arranged as direct payments under **sections 50** or **52**

(Direct payments) of the Act, to a person for up to 6 weeks to enable them to maintain or regain their ability to live independently at home.

- care and support provided to those with Creutzfeldt-Jacob Disease;
- after-care services/support provided under **section 117 of the Mental Health Act** 1983 (see the explanation at Chapter 6.1);
- the processes involved in assessing and providing services, as opposed to the services themselves. This includes the provision of information and advice;
- transport to a day service where the transport is provided as part of meeting a person's needs;

independent professional advocacy where a local authority has arranged for the provision of this in accordance with the code of practice on advocacy under Part 10 (Complaints, Representatives and Advocacy Services) of the Ac.

In certain circumstances there is no obligation to carry out a financial assessment. These are:-

- where the local authority makes a flat rate charge (e.g. for preventative services) and it would be disproportionate to the effort involved to make a charge;
- where the person provides only limited information; in such a case, the authority may base their charge on such information as they have, if they are able to do so;

- where the person is receiving care and support for which no charge can be made.

The authority must follow the regulations when carrying out the means test.

There is a maximum weekly charge, which is set by regulations. At the time of writing, this is £90 per week.

6.2.7 Disregard of personal injury payments

The **Care and Support (Financial Assessment) (Wales) Regulations 2015** provide for capital and income sums to be disregarded in calculating the amount of any charge. **Schedule 2** provides for the following items of capital to be disregarded:-

> ***14.*** *Any amount which would be disregarded under paragraph 12 of Schedule 10 to the Income Support Regulations (personal injury trusts).*
>
> ***15.*** *Any amount which would be disregarded under paragraph 12A of Schedule 10 to the Income Support Regulations (personal injury payments) with the exception of any payment or any part of any payment that has been specifically identified by a court to deal with the cost of providing care.*

Similarly, in Schedule 1, the Welsh regulations mirror the English regulations by providing for the following to be disregarded:-

> ***14.**—(1) … any relevant payment made or due to be made at regular intervals …*
>
> *(2) … any relevant payment made or due to be made at regular intervals which is intended and used for any item which was not taken into account when assessing the reasonable cost of meeting or securing A's need for care and support.*
>
> *(3) In this paragraph, "relevant payment" … means—*
>
> > …
> >
> > *(c) a payment … from a trust whose funds are derived from a payment made in consequence of any personal injury to A;*
> >
> > *(d) a payment under an annuity purchased—*
> >
> > > *(i) pursuant to any agreement or court order to make payments to A; or*
> > >
> > > *(ii) from funds derived from a payment made,*
> >
> > *in consequence of any personal injury to A;*
> >
> > *(e) a payment (not falling within paragraphs (a) to (d)) received by virtue of any agreement or court order to make payments to A in consequence of any personal injury to A*

Again, therefore, the setting up of a personal injury trust will have the effect of sheltering the compensation from any effect on the cost to the individual of any care provided by or through the local authority.

6.3 Does the local authority or the tortfeasor pay?

Issues may arise as to the relationship between the duties of both English and Welsh local authorities referred to above and the inclusion in a damages award of a sum of money to provide for similar care functions in the future. The most recent authority is that of the Court of Appeal in **Peters (by her litigation friend, Susan Miles) v East Midlands Strategic Health Authority & Nottingham City Council [2009] EWCA Civ 145 (3 March 2009).**

Local authorities have a duty, now under the Care Act 2014, to meet the needs for care and support which are identified by an assessment. Previously the duty was to provide domiciliary care, or as in the instant case accommodation under section 21 of the **National Assistance Act 1948**, for those with severe disabilities, which is likely to include the victims of serious accidents. The authority was previously under a further duty to charge for such accommodation under **sec 22** of the **National Assistance Act,** and under the **Care Act section 14** has a discretion to do so.

Under the former rules, the receipt of a capital sum which took the injured party's capital to more than the capital limit would have meant that they would be required to pay for the whole of their accommodation. However, the change in rules in 1998 to permit certain sums of personal injury compensation to be disregarded, including payments administered by the Court of Protection, meant that such a person might well be entitled to be placed in accommodation for which the local authority would be required to pay.

One perhaps unintended consequence of the changes was to lead to the argument that there was no longer any need for awards of damages for long term care where a local authority would in any event be under a duty to provide that care free of charge. Any compensation for this purpose would have to be ignored by the local authority, and it would be extremely unlikely that it would be used to pay for residential care, so such a payment might be regarded as unjust enrichment. The effect would therefore be to pass the burden of funding long term care for an accident victim from the wrongdoer to the local authority.

There are three reasons why the issue of local authority care is relevant in any event. The first is that the injured party may need to rely on this pending the establishment of liability (which of course may not ultimately be established). The second is that community care may be needed to 'top up' a defendant's liability, for example if there is contributory negligence. The third is that the claimant may need or wish to use community care in any event.

The instant case was a medical negligence case in which the NHS admitted liability and the only issue was the quantum of damages. The NHS argued that they should not be expected to pay for the cost of accommodation as this would be provided free by the local authority. The High Court rejected their argument and awarded the claimant £3.8 million in respect of future accommodation and care costs. The NHS appealed.

The Court of Appeal upheld the judge at first instance and held that the claimant had the right in effect to decline local authority provision and to receive damages to cover her future care and accommodation, rather than relying on a lifetime provision by the local authority. The Court said,

> "*provided that there was no real risk of double recovery, the [High Court] was right to hold that there was no reason in principle why the claimant should give up her right to damages to meet her wish to pay for her care needs herself rather than to become dependent on the State.*"

The risk of double recovery arises because the claimant could in theory take the money awarded by the Court and then later resort to the local authority for care. The Court found that the presence of a Court of Protection appointed deputy meant that the risk of double recovery could be avoided. The deputy undertook to approach the Court of Protection and to ask for a variation in the terms of her appointment so that she could not approach the local authority for funding without the approval of the Court of Protection, who would also have to give notice to the defendant in the present case. The Court of Appeal said:

> "*In our judgment, this is an effective way of dealing with the risk of double recovery in cases where the affairs of the claimant are being administered by the Court of Protection. It places the control over the Deputy's ability to make an application for the provision of a claimant's care and accommodation at public expense in the hands of a court. If a Deputy wishes to apply for public provision even where damages have been awarded on the basis that no public provision will be sought, the requirement that the defendant is to be notified of*

any such application will enable a defendant who wishes to do so to seek to persuade that the Court of Protection should not allow the application to be made because it is unnecessary and contrary to the intendment of the assessment of damages. The court accordingly accepts the undertaking that has been offered".

The Court of Appeal recognised that its conclusion in this case may be difficult to reconcile with its earlier decision in **Sowden v Lodge [2004] EWCA Civ 1370**. The Court in the present case sought to distinguish it on the ground that no binding ruling on the point was made in the earlier case. It is perhaps worth noting that the Court in the present case was a particularly strong Court of Appeal (the Master of the Rolls, the President of the Queen's Bench Division, and Dyson LJ as he then was); and also that Pill LJ, in giving judgement in **Sowden v Lodge**, noted that McGregor on Damages (17th edition) strongly argued that it should be for the tortfeasor, and not the local authority, to pay.

A slightly different issue arose in the case of **Tinsley v Manchester City Council [2017] EWCA Civ 1704.** Here the issue was whether the local authority could, in effect, avoid its liability to provide after-care services under **Section 117 Mental Health Act 1983**, on the basis that, as argued by the local authority in the Court of Appeal:

1. on a proper construction of section 117 the local authority is not required to provide aftercare services to a person who has received damages for their future care; and
2. to allow free aftercare where there was such an award would offend the principle of double recovery – the claimant having

received damages to pay for care which later had to be provided for free.

The Court of Appeal held that they could not. The first argument was impossible in the light of the decision of the House of Lords in **Stennett** (see above para 6.1). While recognising the concerns of the local authority with regard to the second point, Longmore LJ, giving the judgement of the Court, approved the undertakings given by the deputy in **Peters v EMSHA** as a way of preventing double recovery, and suggested that in reality most people would not turn to local authority support while they have the option of funding their care privately.

CHAPTER SEVEN
NHS CONTINUING HEALTH CARE

7.1 Paying for health care services

Whereas NHS care is free at the point of use, care provided by local authorities is subject to charge under the **Care Act 2014** in England and the **Social Services and Well-Being (Wales) Act 2014** in Wales. There continues to be a distinction drawn between health and social care, and where the distinction lies has been subject to a number of challenges.

In **R v North and East Devon Health Authority ex parte Coughlan [2000] 2 WLR 622**, following a catastrophic accident in which she was knocked from her bike, the disabled person was firstly accommodated in a hospital, and then subsequently in a long stay facility provided by the NHS. When that facility was closed, she was relocated into independent accommodation with services provided by the local authority. The dispute centred on eligibility criteria agreed between the health authority and the local authority as to what services constituted health care (free at the point of use) and what constituted social care (provided by the local authority and therefore chargeable). The Court of Appeal held that social services could only fund low level nursing care. The eligibility criteria could not impose on the local authority a responsibility which goes beyond their powers; and the criteria as established were therefore unlawful.

Fresh guidance was issued (**HSC 2001/015: LAC (2001) 18**). The system of the Registered Nursing Care Contribution was introduced, which enabled the provision by the NHS of a contribution towards the nursing needs of those living in a nursing home, but this was no more than sticking plaster (although it is still in place). Reliance on the guidance could give rise to a gap between local authority and health entitlements, as noted by the judge in **R (T, D and B) v Haringey LBC [2005] EWHC 2235 (Admin)**, and this gap was addressed directly in the case of **R (Grogan) v Bexley NHS Care Trust [2006] EWHC 44 (Admin)**, which heavily criticised the guidance mentioned above.

As a consequence the National Framework for Continuing Health Care was issued in England in June 2007. The Welsh equivalent was issued in 2010. The current editions are October 2018 in England, and 2014 in Wales.

7.2 The Alternatives

Where a person receives any kind of care, it is necessary to determine how the cost is to be met. There are three alternatives:-

- NHS continuing health care – funded by the state.
- Funded nursing care – also funded by the state, but only to a specific degree.
- Care paid for by the individual, with support from the local authority.

7.3 Continuing Health Care

7.3.1 What it is

> "***NHS Continuing Healthcare*** *means a package of ongoing care that is arranged and funded solely by the National Health Service (NHS) where the individual has been assessed and found to have a 'primary health need' as set out in [the 2018] National Framework."*
>
> *(English National Framework 2018 page 7)*

Clinical Commissioning Groups are responsible for promoting awareness of the policy in England, and for ensuring that it is properly implemented, and for determining eligibility. Care can be provided in any setting, including a patient's own home or a care home. If the person is eligible, the CCG arranges funds for care. In Wales, Local Health Boards are responsible for implementing the policy, and deciding eligibility. If the person is eligible, the LHB arranges funds for care.

The English National Framework and Practice Guidance can be found on the Gov.UK website at https://www.gov.uk/government/publications/national-framework-for-nhs-continuing-healthcare-and-nhs-funded-nursing-care

The Welsh Framework can be found at via the link Continuing NHS Healthcare The National Framework for Implementation in Wales 2014

7.3.2 Assessment

Consent should be sought before the assessment takes place. The patient can choose a family member or other person to advocate on their behalf. (Guidance paras 33-35).

If the patient lacks capacity to consent, it should be determined whether any other person (such as an Attorney) has the responsibility for giving consent under the provisions of the **Mental Capacity Act 2005,** or whether the patient has made an Advance Decision. If not, then action must be taken in the patient's best interests. If the patient lacks capacity, and there is no appropriate relative or carer to be consulted, then consideration should be given to the appointment of an Independent Mental Capacity Advocate (IMCA), in cases where serious medical treatment or change of accommodation is proposed.

The legal basis of CHC is section 3 of the NHS Act 2006. CHC is a combination of medical services (section 3(1)(c)), non-hospital accommodation (section 3(1)(b)), and other services (section 3(1)(e)). It may be noted that the power to provide accommodation is limited to accommodation for the purpose of the provision of service and is not a general power to provide accommodation: **R (Whapples) v Birmingham Crosscity Clinical Commissioning Group [2015] EWCA Civ 435.**

7.3.3 Procedure

The full assessment is carried out using the matrix below, which is taken from page 42 of the NHS Framework for Continuing Health Care which can be found via https://www.gov.uk/government/publications/national-framework-for-nhs-continuing-healthcare-and-nhs-funded-nursing-care. Pending a full assessment, there will usually be a shorter form of assessment to ascertain the likelihood of the patient qualifying for CHC.

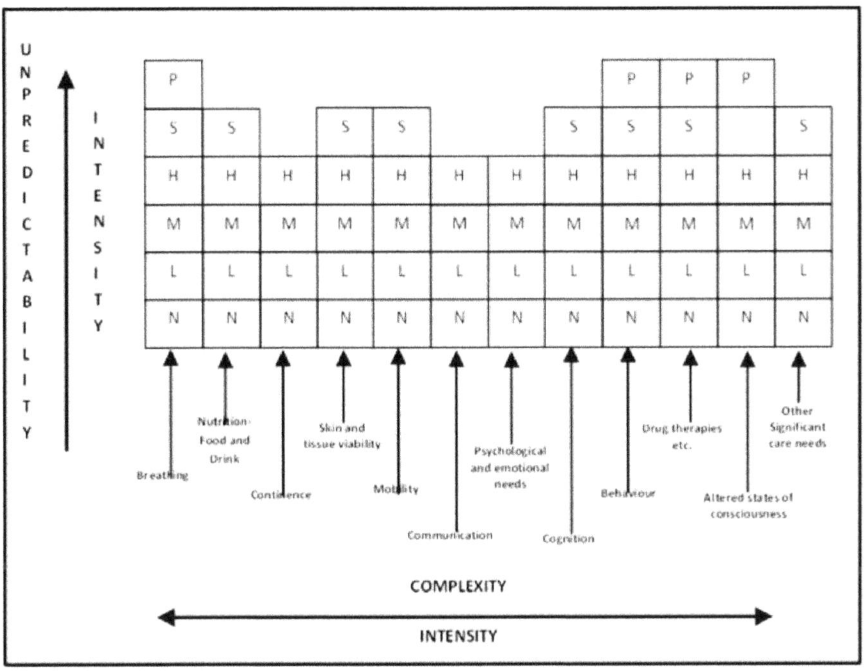

P is priority, S is severe, H is high, M is moderate, L is low and N is none. The needs of the person are considered in respect of each of the above "domains". The result is not an arithmetical exercise, but rather based on the pattern of outcomes – one or two priority needs may well lead to a finding in favour of continuing health care, but so might say six severe findings or eight or nine high findings. It is the overall results that determine whether or not the person is likely to qualify.

The full assessment is carried out by way of the Decision Support Tool, which is a statutory document. The decision is taken by a multi-disciplinary team, who are intended as the experts in the process. Their recommendation goes to the CCG, who decide; but they are required to follow the MDT except in "exceptional circumstances". The CCG should not merely substitute its own findings for those of the MDT. "Exceptional circumstances" are listed in Practice Guidance Note 39, and include where the DST is not completed properly; where there are evidential gaps; where there is an obvious mismatch between evidence and the recommendation; and where the recommendation would result in either authority acting unlawfully. In all such cases, the CCG should refer the matter back to the MDT and ask them to address the issues found.

The result will be a recommendation as to whether or not continuing heath care should be awarded. If it is, the next issue is where the person should live; i.e. the type of accommodation should not be a determining factor. If continuing health care is awarded, the whole of the person's care needs will be met by the NHS.

It should be noted that the notes above refer to the system in England. Wales is subject to its own regime, and while the basic system in Wales is the same, there are differences, and reference should be made to the links to the Welsh system referred to above.

7.4 Funded nursing care

Local authorities are prevented from providing nursing care by **section 49** of the **Health and Social Care Act 2001.** Where a resident of a nursing home has a care need, therefore, it will be necessary to determine how the care is to be provided.

If the need is a 'primary need' for nursing care, the full costs of providing all that resident's care (nursing and non-nursing) are borne by the NHS under the continuing health care provisions. Where the resident requires some nursing care, but nursing is not his or her primary need, the NHS will pay only part of the care costs. This contribution is known as 'Funded Nursing Care' ("FNC"). FNC is a contribution which is laid down in regulations. In 2019/20 the rate in England is £165.56 per week at the standard rate, with the higher rate available to certain longstanding recipients of care being set at £227.77. In Wales, the figure is £179.97.

In such a case, dependent upon means, the resident in question and/or the relevant local authority is responsible for paying for the remainder of the care costs.

Recently the courts have considered the interface between these two positions. The case is a Welsh one and is concerned with Welsh Local Health Boards, but the case, it is submitted, is of more general application.

The specific issue was what was being paid for by the NHS – just the actual nursing care, or ancillary matters as well? In **R (Forge Care Homes Ltd & Ors) v Cardiff and Vale University Health Board & Ors [2017] UKSC 56** a unanimous Supreme Court held that nursing care by a registered nurse covered not just the act of nursing but also the ancillary functions, all of which therefore fell to be paid for in the Funded Nursing Care Contribution by the NHS. Giving the judgement of the Court, Lady Hale, at paragraph 44, said,

> "*In my view, therefore, "nursing care by a registered nurse" covers (a) time spent on nursing care, in the sense of care which can only be provided by a registered nurse, including both direct and indirect nursing time as defined by the Laing and Buisson study; (b) paid breaks; (c) time receiving supervision; (d) stand-by time; and (e) time spent on providing, planning, supervising or delegating the provision of other types of care which in all the circumstances ought to be provided by a registered nurse because they are ancillary to or closely connected with or part and parcel of the nursing care which she has to provide.*"

CHAPTER EIGHT
TYPES OF PERSONAL INJURY TRUST

8.1 Introduction

Although as noted above the type of trust is irrelevant as far as the disregard of capital for benefit purposes is concerned, other factors may intervene to determine whether a bare trust will suffice, or whether some other form of trust might be considered. Factors may include taxation. Although in many cases this is not an issue, nevertheless care should be taken to ensure that the decision as to the appropriate form of trust does not lead to unexpected charges to inheritance tax or capital gains tax. The tax implications of each of the types of trust are considered below.

8.2 Bare Trusts

This is the simplest form of trust. Property is given to trustees to hold for a beneficiary or beneficiaries absolutely. Usually the beneficiary is him- or herself the settlor.

In a bare trust, the beneficiary may call for the assets at any time. However, the trustees still have duties as trustees, and are not under an obligation to pay money over for inappropriate purposes.

It is not an obstacle that the beneficiary is mentally incapable. The Court of Protection can (and commonly will) authorise a Deputy to sign a trust deed. Similarly, a trust can be established for a minor.

The trustees need to be unanimous in their decision making. Normally, payments out of the trust can be organised simply by the trustees signing a cheque. Ultimately, the mentally capable beneficiary can bring the trust to an end ('bust the trust') by insisting that all assets are transferred to him or her.

Note that there is a distinction between a bare trust and money held in a solicitor's client account. Money in a client account belongs to the client, and can be accessed on demand. Where the property is in a trust, the injured settlor still has to obtain the permission of the trustees to hand the money over. See the case of **CIS368/1994**, in which the Social Security Commissioner said

> "*In my view the use of the word 'trust' should be understood in simple terms, used to cover the situation where the legal estate is in one person but the beneficial estate is in another person.*"

It will therefore be appreciated that the key point is the question of whether the legal and beneficial estates are vested in the same person. So long as they are not, then it is likely that the trust will be efficient for benefits purposes.

8.3 Life Interest Trusts

A Life Interest Trust is commonly described as a 'flexible life interest trust'. The assets are held by trustees, but the injured settlor is established as the 'life tenant', i.e. he or she receives the trust income for life. It would be normal for the settlor in this situation also to be entitled to benefit from capital payments during the course of the trust, and it would be usual for the trust to contain 'wide powers of appointment' to achieve this. The major difference from the bare trust is that this type of trust permits disposal of the trust assets to a third party on the death of the injured settlor.

Although, therefore, there is no obstacle to setting up a personal injury trust along these lines, and although such a trust will still attract the benefit capital disregards discussed above, this does not mean that tax will not be a consideration, and the complexities of the tax regime must be considered. The assets of the trust will pass on death, and so be likely to be chargeable to inheritance tax.

There are other issues to be considered. It is unlikely that a mentally incapable beneficiary can establish a flexible life interest trust. The view of the Court of Protection is likely to be that, whereas a bare trust has no dispositive effect, a life interest trust seeks to dispose of the property on the death of the settlor, and the Court of Protection may have objections to the assets being disposed of as this may not be in the best interests of the settlor.

In the case of a life interest trust, the settlor can normally appoint the initial and any replacement trustees during their lifetime. After their death, that power will be vested in the trustees.

Unlike a bare trust, the settlor has no right to call for the assets in the trust fund. The trustees owe a duty, not just to the settlor/life tenant, but also to the remaindermen.

On the death of the settlor, the property will pass in accordance with the terms of the trust. It will not pass either under the settlor's Will or under the rules on intestacy.

8.4 Discretionary Trusts

Under a discretionary trust, no individual beneficiary has any right to receive any of the trust property. The trust deed will set out the class of beneficiaries, and it is a matter for the trustees as to what they pay and to whom.

The rules on accumulations apply; income will have to be paid out after the expiry of the maximum 21 year legal income accumulation period, unless the settlor's lifetime is used as the accumulation period in the alternative. This would almost certainly be preferable.

The trust deed will set a period which is the period for the longest lawful life of the trust. It is usual for this to be a period of 80 years less 1 day, although if it is a feasible option for the trust to determine on the settlor's death, then it may be appropriate to use the settlor's life as the period for which the trust will exist. Of course if this procedure is followed, it will be necessary to consider other beneficiaries.

Since the Court of Protection is unlikely to accept a trust which gives wide powers of disposition to trustees, for practical purposes it may be assumed that only a mentally capable settlor can affect a discretionary trust.

The powers of the trustees will be similar to those in life interest or bare trusts. Because the trust is discretionary, they will have the powers to make advances of income or capital. They will also have the power to purchase items for the beneficiaries. As usual, all decisions of the trustees must be unanimous.

New trustees will normally be appointed by the continuing trustees.

If it is desired to secure continuing means tested benefits entitlement for beneficiaries of the settlor, then the discretionary trust is the most effective way of doing so. A discretionary trust gives no outright entitlement to the beneficiary, who is thus not entitled to call for any payments from the fund, and the trust assets will therefore be disregarded as capital when their means tested benefits are assessed.

8.5 Trusts for Mentally Capable Minors

Where the injured person is a mentally capable minor, the most appropriate form of personal injury trust is a bare trust. This would be created by the Court under CPR 21.11. This would ensure that nobody else can benefit from the compensated minor's money before they reach the age of 18, and also that the minor can bring an end to the trust when they reach that age if they so choose. They do not have to do so, and their position as regards means tested benefits is unlikely to be a determining factor. The trust should therefore not be determined automatically at 18.

Since the money in the trust belongs to the minor, and the purpose of the trust is to enable its administration during the minority, Coldrick argues that the court has no power to defer the age of vesting until an age greater than 18. See Coldrick on Personal Injury Trusts (4th edition), 2008, page 27.

In a personal injury case the court will normally appoint a litigation friend for the minor. The litigation friend, however, is not empowered to agree the terms of the trust. That can only be done by the court. The court is likely to wish to be informed of the proposals for the management of the award, and this would normally include a report from the trust lawyer and a financial adviser.

The power to remove trustees can only be exercised by an order of the court. The power of appointing new trustees is normally invested in the on-going trustees.

If the minor dies before the age of 18, then intestacy rules will apply. Once he or she reaches 18, then a Will can be employed to determine the destination for the trust fund on the death of the settlor.

8.6 Section 89 IHTA Trusts for Disabled People

One of the options which may be open to a person who meets a particular definition of disability is that of a trust which takes advantage of the provisions of **Section 89 Inheritance Act 1984** as amended by the **Finance Act 2006**.

The original purpose of Section 89 trusts was to enable a person to make provision for a disabled person by way of setting up a trust. Such a trust would attract tax advantages; a transfer into it is treated for tax purposes as a potentially exempt transfer, and the trusts are also exempt from the ten year and exit charges. The funds in the trust do, however, aggregate to the estate of the disabled person on his or her death. If the trust is self-settled, then this would in any event be likely to be academic, in view of the 'gift with reservation' rules which would require a gift in which the donor retains an interest to be treated as still part of their estate. However, original Section 89 trusts do not carry income or capital gains tax advantages, which have therefore always rendered them less popular than flexible life interest trusts.

Although an original section 89 trust can still be established, the Finance Act 2006 extended the scope of this kind of trust by adding various additional types of trust to the regime, which makes them potentially more attractive. However, there are some potential difficulties with the new rules.

8.6.1. Disabled people

In order to establish a Section 89 trust, a 'disabled' person must be involved. He or she is so defined (by **section 89(6)**, and by **Schedule 1A to the Finance Act 2005**) by reference to one of six possible conditions. These are that the disabled person is:-

- Incapable by reason of mental disorder within the **Mental Health Act 1983** of administering his/her property or managing his/her affairs.
- The **Mental Health Act 1983** was amended by the **Mental Health Act 2007,** which extended the definition of 'mental disorder' to mean 'any disorder or disability of the mind'. This is a significantly wider definition than that contained in the **Mental**

Health Act 1983 as unamended, and covers a wide range of possible mental conditions. Many of the people covered by this section may (but will not necessarily) come under the auspices of the Court of Protection. Note, however, that lack of mental capacity by itself is not sufficient for a person to meet this definition of disability.

- In receipt of attendance allowance;
- In receipt of the daily living component of personal independence payment, or the higher or middle rate care component of disability living allowance;

In receipt of an increased disablement pension (it is not clear what type of disablement pension is meant here);

In receipt of an armed forces independence payment; and/or

In receipt of an industrial injury constant attendance allowance.

It is understood that HMRC will accept that a person with certain specified conditions thereby meets the first of these conditions. The qualifying conditions are:

- Alzheimer's or other forms of dementia;
- Bipolar disorder, schizophrenia, depression, or other mental illness;
- Autistic Spectrum Disorder (sometimes described as a pervasive developmental disorder);

- a learning disability, such as Down's Syndrome.

Attendance allowance and disability living allowance (DLA) are variations on the same benefit, which is intended to provide extra income for someone with a disability (see Chapter 5). Personal independence payment (PIP) replaces DLA for new claims.

The difference between attendance allowance and PIP/DLA is the age at which a claim is made. Attendance allowance is the benefit for those whose claim is made on or after they reach pension age, while DLA and PIP are for those who claim before that age. As noted above, no new claims for DLA can be considered except for those under the age of 16, but this may give entitlement to access to the trusts being considered here, so reference should be made to the detailed conditions for DLA as outlined in Chapter 5, where the detailed conditions for attendance allowance (which overlaps with DLA) are also considered. For the purposes of the definition, the conditions for DLA and for attendance allowance are identical. They may be summarised as follows. The disabled person must be so severely disabled as to require -

- care and attention by day in connection with his or her bodily functions; or
- care and attention at night in connection with his or her bodily functions; or
- continual supervision in order to avoid substantial danger to him or herself or to others during the day; or
- someone to be awake at night for the purpose of watching over them.

Someone in receipt of the higher mobility component of DLA will also qualify. This will cover those under 16, and also those who had originally successfully claimed DLA as adults but who have not yet been transferred to PIP

The higher mobility component is payable to someone who cannot walk, or for whom the effort of walking is so significant that they can be described as virtually unable to walk. Again, this is explained in more detail in Chapter 5.

Personal Independence Payment is in the process of replacing DLA, with the express intention of cutting costs. Those who were claiming DLA before the changeover will (over a period of time) be assessed for entitlement to PIP, and will be transferred to PIP if they qualify. It is expected that not all those who previously qualified for DLA would be transferred to PIP, and a significant number would be told that they no longer qualify. This may mean that a person who qualified as the beneficiary of a section 89 trust at one point in time may not at a later stage actually be receiving a qualifying benefit. In principle this should not matter, as long as the person is entitled to the relevant benefit at the time the trust is set up. It might, however, be problematic if a recipient of DLA were to be reassessed while the trust was in process of being set up, with the result of losing his or her qualifying benefit.

Where a disabled person does not meet the criteria for any of the benefits, either because he or she lives outside the UK, or because he or she lives in accommodation where the relevant benefits are not available, he or she can nevertheless be deemed to meet the conditions for the purposes of a section 89 trust. This will require an independent assessment of the person, since the Department for Work and Pensions will not carry out such an assessment because the person does not qualify for the benefit. Note that the person will not be deemed in receipt of the benefit if he or she is absent from the UK, or is in prison.

Where the disabled person is under the auspices of the Court of Protection, it is unlikely that the court will countenance the setting up of a Section 89 trust except under unusual circumstances (see chapter 10). Such trusts are, however, used by the Criminal Injuries Compensation Authority, particularly in cases involving children who were injured by their parents. This ensures that the parents will not benefit under the intestacy rules on the death of a child. The Court of Protection is more likely simply to set up a bare trust. Because the injured person is not mentally capable, he or she is not able to bring the trust to an end without the authority of the court. It is also possible to put in place a statutory will to deal with any remaining trust fund at death. This arrangement may also enable the retention of a spousal exemption to inheritance tax.

8.6.2. Original section 89 trusts

The significance of a section 89 trust now is its tax advantages; these are acquired by mans of a "vulnerable persons election" and this may apply to any of the forms of trust previously considered. The aim is to enable someone to make provision for a vulnerable disabled child, or any other person who is mentally and physically disabled.

The form of trust required is discretionary, with accumulation of income while that is possible. The accumulation period would normally be the lifetime of the settlor, rather than 21 years, unless the settlor is not expected to live for very long. This type of trust ensures that no interest in possession exists.

8.6.3 New section 89A and 89B IHTA trusts

The **Finance Act 2006** introduced new types of sec 89 trusts under **sections 89A and 89B. Section 89A** allows for a wider group of disabled people to be subject to such a trust. **Section 89B(1)(d)** allows certain post 21st March 2006 interest in possession trusts to fall within the definition of a 'disabled person's interest' in a similar manner. This also enabled, among other things, a settlor to set up a trust in anticipation of meeting one or more of the conditions later; this may not be a relevant consideration in most personal injury cases, but should be borne in mind in the event of later deterioration.

Both types of trust are intended to allow a person whose health is deteriorating, or is likely to do so, to put a trust in place to administer their own affairs. This is so even though the original conditions of a sec 89 trust cannot be fulfilled at the time of founding the trust. .

8.7 Choosing the Type of Trust

For a mentally capable adult beneficiary, a bare trust is the simplest and most cost effective way of meeting the requirements. It will be possible to create a different type of trust at a later stage if circumstances changed. Because the proceeds of the award were immediately placed into trust, the benefits disregard will apply ab initio. Changing to another type of trust at a later stage would not affect benefit entitlement.

If the injured person is mentally incapable, whether an adult or a child, then it will be for the Court of Protection to determine the type of trust required. In almost all cases this will be a bare trust.

If the injured person is a mentally capable minor, then it is considered that a bare trust created by the High Court under CPR 21.11 is the only lawful and appropriate way of setting up a trust.

This would seem to indicate that a bare trust is likely to be the most appropriate scenario in the majority of cases. It now becomes necessary to consider the situations in which other types of trust should be considered.

8.7.1 The Vulnerable Beneficiary

The beneficiary is not mentally incapable, but is sufficiently self-aware to appreciate that he or she is liable to spend any money which is placed under his or her control. Placing the money in a trust will avoid this. It may be appropriate in such a case to seek to set up a discretionary trust.

8.7.2 People Subject to Third Party Pressure

There may be circumstances where the potential beneficiary is him or herself vulnerable to exploitation by others, either in his or her business life, or with members of the family, and it would be safer to set up a life interest or discretionary arrangement to prevent the (potential) exploiter gaining access to the funds.

8.7.3 A Person with Heirs

The settlor may wish to protect his or her potential heirs who are receiving means tested benefits, or who should not receive money outright for other reasons. In such a case it would be possible to set up a discretionary trust to deal with the problem. It might, however, be more appropriate to consider a bare trust during the settlor's life, backed up by a discretionary will trust. If the settlor needs to set up a more protective type of arrangement, then the key question will often be whether the settlor's estate on death is likely to exceed the nil rate band. If it is not, then it may be purely a matter of practicality as to which type of trust is chosen. If it is likely to exceed that level, there are considerable complications which need to be addressed with care.

8.8 Drafting and administrative considerations

Once the type of trust has been decided, the trust deed may be drafted. There are numerous precedents available, and practitioners will not need to be reminded to ensure the suitability and accuracy of the trust deed from the taxation point of view. Some basic drafting principles may stand repetition:-

- Clearly identify the trust by its name
- Use clear and easy to follow definitions and apply them consistently
- Include recitals to explain the background to the trust

- Define the trust fund clearly, and ensure that it is only the personal injury compensation that is paid into the trust
- STEP (The Society of Trust and Estate Practitioners) provide a standard set of administration provisions which it may be suitable to incorporate
- There is no longer a requirement to certify for stamp duty.

The Trustees will need to prepare accounts on an annual basis, and should in addition meet annually and minute their deliberations. Trust tax returns may be required.

Do not lose sight of the settlor's benefits and entitlement to local authority services, and ensure so far as possible that the settlor notifies the DWP promptly of any change in circumstances. Ensure that the settlor's will is kept up to date, and that the need for a power of attorney and/or a deputyship is also kept under review if these are not in place at the outset.

8.9 The tax position of different types of trust

This is considered in outline only, and specialist advice should be sought in appropriate cases.

The taxes to be taken into account are inheritance tax, income tax and inheritance tax. The inheritance tax nil rate band should be considered in the case of an award in excess of that amount – currently £325,000. If such a sum is invested in a relevant property trust – a discretionary or life interest trust – there is an immediate charge to inheritance tax at 20% on the amount exceeding the nil rate band. (If the person concerned has unused annual exemptions going back for a period of no more than a year, the figure might be increased to £331,000.)

The case of **Pitt v Holt [2013] UKSC 26** is instructive and serves as a warning. The case concerned compensation payable to Derek Pitt, who suffered catastrophic injuries in a road accident, including a loss of mental capacity. The case was settled for an amount in the region of £1.2m, and the compensation was placed by Mr Pitt's receiver, his wife Patricia, into a discretionary trust, the terms of which were approved by the Court of Protection. Advice had been sought and given prior to settling the property into a trust, but the advice overlooked the issue of inheritance tax, as did the Court of Protection, who did not consider the possibility of a sec 89 trust. Use of such a trust would have overcome the problem which then arose, which was an immediate charge to tax at the rate of 20% on the sum which exceeded the nil rate band. One of the issues before the Supreme Court was therefore whether it was possible to set the settlement aside as a consequence, on the basis of mistake.

Where the settlement is made by use of a sec 89 trust, the 20% inheritance tax charge does not apply. For sec 89 to be appropriate, the beneficiary must qualify as a vulnerable person as outlined above, and an appropriate vulnerable person's election, applicable for that year, must be made.

The income tax and capital gains tax position differs for the various forms of trust. A bare trust is not a "settlement" for tax purposes. It does not have to be registered with HMRC or with the Capital Taxes Office. The income and capital gains are treated as the income and capital gains of the settlor or beneficiary. (See **Section 624 Income Tax (Trading and Other Income) Act 2005** and **Schedule 2 para 5 of the Finance Act 2008** amending the **Taxation of Chargeable Gains Act 1992**).

Because the income and capital gains belong, and continue to belong, to the beneficiary, this arrangement therefore has no tax implications. The proceeds of the trust also still belong to the beneficiary. On the death of the settlor (as injured party), the trust fund forms part of his or her estate and will be distributed in accordance with their Will or the intestacy rules.

The assets in a bare trust also benefit from a capital gains tax free uplift on the death of the settlor.

On the death of the settlor, the normal inheritance tax rules will apply. It follows that under the spousal exemption for inheritance tax, the settlor's spouse or civil partner can inherit the trust fund without being liable to inheritance tax, provided that they inherit outright or under an 'immediate post death interest'.

A court approved bare trust is tax neutral, and has the same tax position as a bare trust for an adult. However, in order to avoid the possibility of the relevant property regime applying for inheritance tax purposes, and thus an accidental charge to inheritance tax being incurred, it is important that the trust instrument should exclude the power to accumulate income under **Section 31(1)** of the **Trustee Act 1925**.

A discretionary trust has its own separate existence, and must be registered with HMRC. If the income falls within the "standard rate band", there are lower rates on the first £1,000 of income. Otherwise, the discretionary trust will be required to pay income tax at the rate applicable to trusts, which is 38.1% for dividends and 45% for other income (England and Wales rates, 2019/20). Since the settlor is interested in the trust, it may be possible to reclaim some of the tax paid by the trustees on their own tax return.

On the death of the injured settlor, there is no capital gains tax free uplift. The trust pays CGT at the rate of 20%, or 28% in the case of residential property. The trust has only half of the personal CGT allowance, which is £6,000 for 2019/20,

In the case of both the bare trust and the life interest trust, tax refunds obtained by the settlor in respect of trust interest may be paid back into the trust without any adverse effect on the benefits position.

Life interest trusts also have a separate identity and must be registered with HMRC. Income tax is generally paid at the basic rate, i.e. 7.5% for dividends and 20% for everything else. In a straightforward case HMRC may agree to waiving a return for the trust and to accepting a declaration by way of the beneficiary's own tax return, but this will not always be applicable.

The treatment of the trust for capital gains tax purposes will be the same as for a discretionary trust. There is, however, one potential issue with capital gains tax, due to the Finance Act 2006. In the case of a life interest trust formed before 22 March 2006, there will be a capital gains tax free uplift on death. However, where the trust was founded after that date, sales of assets which have increased in value may trigger a charge to capital gains tax. This may be mitigated by way of holdover relief which enables the charge to capital gains to be deferred upon vesting. However, the precise implications of what is proposed should be examined as part of the process of determining the type of trust to be entered into.

Otherwise, a trust founded after that date will fall within the relevant property regime. The trust is entitled to half of a personal CGT allowance (£6,000 for 2019/20) and tax is payable at 20%, or 28% in there is residential property involved.

As noted above, the bare trust has no implications for inheritance tax, other than as part of the settlor's estate. In the case of a life interest trust, however, because the trust assets will pass on the death of the settlor, inheritance tax must be considered. The issue is the amount involved. If the estate, including gifts during the preceding 7 years, does not exceed the nil rate band (£325,000 at the time of writing), then there is no charge to inheritance tax. In addition, the exemption for inheritance tax on property passing to the settlor's spouse will also apply.

Finally, as noted above, in the case of a sec 89 vulnerable person's trust, provided that the conditions are satisfied and an appropriate vulnerable person's election is made, the amount of income tax and CGT payable will be the same as the amount that would have been paid by the vulnerable person if the trust assets had been taxed on them.

A section 89 trust is fundamentally a discretionary type trust, but with a deemed interest in possession. It can be quite complicated to draft and administer. For an injured party, there is no great advantage to forming an original sec 89 trust as opposed to a settlor interested ordinary discretionary trust, but in the larger cases, the IHT attractions are clear – the rules of the 'relevant property regime' do not apply, and there are no lifetime IHT entry charges, exit charges or decennial charges.

An original sec 89 trust bears inheritance tax as part of the taxable estate of the disabled person with the deemed interest in possession. Because of the fundamentally discretionary nature of the trust, the spousal exemption does not apply on the death of the injured settlor, even if the trust comes to an end and the trust fund is paid to the surviving spouse outright.

CHAPTER NINE
THE MENTALLY INCAPABLE CLIENT AND THE COURT OF PROTECTION

In the case of an incapable claimant, the Court of Protection is likely to be involved, and to be concerned not just in the settling of the damages award, but also in respect of its long term investment and management.

Where damages for personal injury are paid, there is often good reason to consider the setting up of a personal injury trust. This may have the effect both of sheltering the damages from any impact they may have on the person's means tested benefits, and also of taking advantage of tax planning arrangements.

Where the recipient of damages is incapacitated, the question arises of whether the appropriate mechanism is a personal injury trust, or an award administered by a deputy. In either case, the effect on means tested benefits is the same, and the issue is the best interests of the injured person.

9.1 PI trust or award administered by the Court?

Re HM: SM v HM [2011] EWHC B30 (COP), [2012] Med LR 449, [2012] WTLR 281

The injured party was a seven year old girl who, as a result of injuries sustained at birth, had cerebral palsy. She was awarded damages against the NHS. However, the damages were substantially discounted – a lump sum of £450,000 with periodical payments of £25,000 per annum increasing to £50,000 on HM attaining the age of 18. The damages were well below HM's potential claim and were the result of a compromise order following advice from leading counsel that the claim had less than a 50% chance of success.

The solicitors acting for HM proposed to set up a personal injury trust, and the final settlement order included a provision that application should be made to the Court of Protection to authorise such an order. The application was duly made, but was rejected by DJ Ashton. He took the view that a deputyship was the appropriate vehicle, that this would be in HM's best interests, and that a PI trust was only likely to be applicable in exceptional cases. HM's mother sought a reconsideration, and the case was reconsidered by HHJ Marshall QC.

Judge Marshall held that a deputyship should always be the starting point, but that this would not prevent the Court authorising a PI trust if this was in P's best interests. She laid down a set of guidelines to be considered and applied in each case to determine what would be the best management structure and what would be in the best interests of P. The guidelines are:-

- The limits of a deputyship regime compared to a settlement
- The ability to deal with totality of the mentally incapacitated person's affairs
- The possibility of having joint deputies

- The availability of a suitable family member as a trustee
- The statutory considerations of managing the mentally incapacitated person's affairs through a deputyship or a trust
- The views of the mentally incapacitated person's carers and those interested in his or her welfare
- Whether a deputyship or trust offered the best protection for the person's assets
- What safeguards were in place to supervise a trustee or deputy
- What degree of protection could be given to the incapacitated person by a trustee in comparison to a deputy
- What structure would achieve be most advantageous for tax for the individual
- Which structure would give the better protection for retaining means-tested benefits
- The comparative cost and expense of a trust to a deputyship
- The availability of budget sums covering the cost of deputyship in any award for personal injury damages
- What was the best structure to oversee costs
- What structure would give the most administrative efficiency
- What structure would give the best investment powers
- Would the future involvement of the Court of Protection be an advantage or a disadvantage
- Would family involvement be increased through the structure of a trust

Applying these guidelines, the judge summarised the position as follows.

> "*The choice between deputyship and trust is emphatically not just an even one. It will never be good enough to argue that a proposed trust structure is, overall, equivalent to or "as good as" the operation of a deputyship order and that there is therefore no reason not to authorise it. There has to be a positive reason to authorise it. If the balance between trust and deputyship is only even, or if any suggested practical advantage is only marginal, that will not suffice. It is for the applicant to prove the existence of a sufficiently clear and significant relative benefit to P so as to justify administering his assets through a private law structure rather than the tailor-made public law scheme of deputyship.*"

She nevertheless held that in the instant case it was in the best interests of P to set up a PI trust. One of the significant factors was that it was likely to be more cost effective, given that the damages had been discounted in the first instance and might not be sufficient to meet HM's lifetime needs. Another factor was the competence of HM's mother who was to act as a trustee. The proposition that the appointment of a deputy is the "default position" was supported in **R (ZYN) v Walsall MBC [2014] PTSR 1356 (HC).** The award was administered by a deputy, who was authorised to draw up to £50,000 a year for the use and benefit of the claimant, without requiring separate Court authority to do so. Walsall, who were providing community care services to ZYN at a weekly cost of £271, sought to charge the claimant with the full cost of care, on the basis that her capital and savings exceeded the capital limit. Counsel's argument that an award administered by a deputy was not the same as an award under the supervision of the Court was rejected. The Court held that administration by a deputy was equated with administration by the Court, and the award was therefore to be disregarded in assessing the claimant's capital and income.

However, the issue of the "default position" was again considered in the case of **Watt v ABC [2016] EWCOP 2532 (02 November 2016)**. In that case, Charles J said,

> " *In my view:*
>
> *1. on a proper analysis SM v HM is not authority for the approach taken before me which was effectively that there is a strong presumption in favour of the appointment of a deputy which must be, and only rarely will be, displaced if the COP is to order that P's property should be held on trust, and in any event*
>
> *2. if and to the extent SM v HM is authority for the existence of a presumption or starting point that must be displaced I do not agree with it.*
>
> *A rebuttable presumption founds an approach to a balancing or weighing exercise under which a result needs to be displaced. It is therefore a starting point to a reasoning process that must be displaced. Naturally, reasoning processes must start somewhere but this does not mean that the chosen start (e.g. the existence of a statutory scheme) provides the result unless it is displaced. So there is a real difference between a starting point for a process of reasoning and a starting point that gives the result unless it is be displaced or rebutted.*

In my view, an approach based on a presumption, or a starting point that must be displaced, as to the result that is in P's best interests runs counter to the underlying rationale and purpose of the MCA and, in particular, of its decision and fact sensitive approach to the application of its best interests test in all the circumstances of a given case.

... In the context of the making of orders that the COP has jurisdiction to make, there is nothing in the MCA that says or has the effect that the result will be "X" unless the factors in favour of another result outweigh those in favour of "X".....

In short, the weighing or balancing of competing factors is at the heart of decision making under the MCA and it does not fit with presumptions, starting points or a bias that have to be displaced".

Charles J also considered that the following points should be taken into account in similar cases:

(1) "The management regime for a substantial award of damages should be considered as soon as is practicable.

(2) This will involve a careful consideration of what the claimant (P) has and does not have the capacity to do and of his or her likely capacity and/or vulnerability in the future. This is relevant to both jurisdictional and best interests issues.

(3) It will also involve the identification of all relevant competing factors and should not proceed on the basis that there is a strong presumption that the COP would appoint a deputy and would not make an order that a trust be created of the award. Rather, it would balance the factors that favour the use of the statutory scheme relating

to deputies (that often found the appointment of a deputy in P's best interests) against the relevant competing factors in that case.

(4) It will also involve the identification of the terms and effects (including taxation) and the costs of those rival possibilities.

(5) Care should be taken to ensure that applications that are not straightforward are not decided by case officers in the COP but are put before judges of the COP.

(6) The possibility of listing case management hearings or the final hearing of QB proceedings before a judge who is also nominated as a COP judge should be considered. However, the potential for conflict between the respective roles of the judge in the two courts (e.g. one arising from a consideration of without prejudice communication in respect of the QB proceedings concerning its settlement that is not agreed or not approved by the COP judge) and the respective jurisdictions of the two courts need to be carefully considered"

9.2 The approach of the Court

There would appear to be three possible scenarios.

1. The claimant has capacity both to litigate and to manage the award. The Court of Protection has no part to play, and there are no obstacles to setting up a PI trust. However, it should be remembered that capacity can fluctuate.
2. The claimant has capacity to litigate but not to manage the award. A PI trust may be suitable, but it would be wise to seek a decla-

ration from the Court of Protection as to whether a PI trust or a deputy is appropriate, as in **HM v SM.**

3. The claimant lacks capacity to litigate or to manage an award. In this case, if the award is comparatively small, it will be managed by the Court; if it is not, then it must be managed either by the donee of an existing power of attorney, or a current Deputy, or the Court must direct the litigation friend to apply for the appointment of a deputy.

9.3. Application of damages and best interests

Re JDS; KGS v JDS (2012) EWHC 302 (COP), (2012) MHLO 4 (SJ Lush)

JDS ("James") has cerebral palsy, due to complications surrounding his birth in 1991. He lives with his parents. James received £2,090,000 in damages from the Brighton and Hove Health Authority. £90,000 of the damages was paid to James's parents in respect of the past care they had given to James. £1,611,222 was attributable to James's future care needs and assessed on the basis of expert medical opinion that James would survive into his forties and fifties. James's life expectancy had been revised from an earlier medical assessment that estimated that he would survive only into his thirties.

James's estate consisted of a property worth £675,000, where he lived with his parents, and an investment portfolio of £1,875,000. His deputy, Kevin Smyth, proposed to transfer £500,000 worth of equity in the property to James' parents by way of declaration of trust, in order to mitigate inheritance tax. He applied to the court for permission to do so. His application was opposed by the Official Solicitor, as James' litigation friend, as he did not consider the transfer to be in James' best interests. The transfer was not approved by DJ Dawson, and the case was adjourned with liberty to restore. On 28 April 2011, Mr Smyth presented a revised proposal to the Court. This would involve the transfer the sum of £325,000 into a flexible power of appointment trust. This would have the effect of saving £130,000 in inheritance tax if James survived by seven years.

The Court was advised that James's outgoings outstripped his income on an annual basis by £32,500, but even if this imbalance occurred for the remainder of his life, he would have at least half a million pounds in investments as well as his main residence without taking into account capital growth. The deputy therefore argued that entering into such a scheme would be in James's best interests, looked at objectively and in accordance with the principles of the **Mental Capacity Act 2005**.

Senior Judge Lush rejected the application. He adopted a two tier approach in determining his judgment. He firstly reviewed the section 4 MCA checklist of factors, adopting a 'balance sheet' test as applied in **Re G (TJ) (2010)** by Morgan J. He then considered whether there was any one factor of 'magnetic importance'. This was a principle followed by Lord Justice Thorpe in the case of **Re A (Medical Treatment: Male Sterilisation) 2000 1 FLR 549** and **Crossley v Crossley (2007) EWCA Civ 149**. This enabled the Senior Judge to consider the advantages and disadvantages of such a scheme, effectively counter balancing the potential gains and losses on the balance sheet. He ruled that the application could only be held to meet the best interests test where there were 'significant advantages'. Furthermore, the Court would have to consider whether any of those factors were of 'magnetic importance' (**Crossley v Crossley (2007)**).

In this instance, he ruled that the factor of 'magnetic importance' was the purpose of the clinical negligence award. Clinical negligence awards are based on life expectancy and the costs of care for that life expectancy. James's life expectancy had increased since he was awarded the damages. The judge ruled that there was no real certainty as to James's life expectancy, and based on this factor alone, any best interests analysis had to be cautious. The priority was to preserve his assets for his future care costs. He also made the point that James's care costs would increase rather than decrease as his parents got older and more third party care was required.

In the later case of **Lomas (Deputy) v AK [2014] EWCOP B11**, the application by the deputy was to allow a gift of £150,000 to be made from a young boy's settlement money to his parents. The purpose of the gift was to allow the parents to purchase a property for their son (AK) in Pakistan and deal with the contractors on site to ensure that it was adapted to meet his needs. Lush SJ allowed the application by ordering that there be an interest free loan, and he distinguished the case from **Re JDS** because the purpose of the gift in that case (inheritance tax planning) was not a purpose for which his award (clinical negligence damages) was intended. In AK's case, the principal purpose was not inheritance planning but rather to ensure that suitable arrangements were made to allow AK's funds to be invested in a property, which could be adapted to meet AK's needs more effectively.

9.4 Overlapping duties and risk of double recovery

In the normal course of events the responsible party might be expected to pay for the costs of care, but how does this fit with the duties of the local authority outlined above? In the case of a client who lacks capacity, the issue has most recently been considered by the Court of Appeal in **Peters (by her litigation friend, Susan Miles) v East Midlands Strategic Health Authority & Nottingham City Council [2009] EWCA Civ 145 (3 March 2009)**, which is considered above at chapter 6.3. The particular relevance here is that the litigation friend in that case was also a Court of Protection appointed deputy.

9.5. Issues of procedure

The jurisdiction of the Court of Protection is laid down by the **Mental Capacity Act 2005**, and covers the welfare and finances of those people who lack capacity to manage their own affairs. The court has power to appoint a deputy to act on behalf of someone who lacks capacity. The deputy need not be the same as the litigation friend, but once a deputy is appointed it would be normal for them to take that role. Otherwise, a litigation friend will need to act on behalf of the injured person in proceedings before the court.

The person who so acts must file a certificate of suitability with the court, which states:-

that he or she consents to act;

- that he or she knows or believes that the claimant lacks capacity, together with a copy of any medical evidence;
- that he or she can fairly and competently conduct the proceedings on behalf of the disabled party;
- that he or she has no conflict of interest with the injured party;
- that he or she will undertake to pay any costs which the disabled person is ordered to pay whilst they are themselves bringing proceedings, subject to any right of recovery that he or she may have from the injured person's assets.

An action cannot be settled or compromised on behalf of the injured person without the consent of the court in which the proceedings are being conducted. Proposals must be in the person's best interests. The consent of the Court of Protection is no longer required to a settlement, and this can be done by the court where the litigation is conducted.

Where asked to approve a settlement on behalf of an incapable person, the court will wish to see counsel's advice recommending the settlement. This should also consider whether a structured settlement is required, and if so the appropriate terms.

Once a case has been settled, an application should be made for the appointment of a deputy as soon as possible. This will not be necessary if the court has already authorised a trust. Where more that £30,000 is recovered on behalf of the injured person, the order approving the settlement will contain the direction that the litigation friend should apply to the Court of Protection for the appointment of a deputy following which the fund will be transferred to the Court of Protection. The appropriate wording for the judgement or order is as follows:-

> *'That the defendant do within days pay the said sum of pounds into court to be placed to and accumulated in a Special Account pending an application by [litigation friend] to the Court of Protection for the appointment of a Deputy for [claimant] and that upon such an appointment being made the said sum of together with interest thereon [subject to a first charge under the Access to Justice Act 1999] be transferred to the Court of Protection to the credit of [claimant] to be dealt with as the Court of Protection thinks fit.'*

Applying for a personal injury trust it is possible to leave the funds with the court and, if desired, to ask the court to approve their external investment. However, clients may prefer to leave the court behind and to set up a trust themselves. This may involve transferring the funds to a personal injury trust. The Court of Protection can approve the application for a PI trust on behalf of the injured person (see **HM v SM**, above). They will only approve it if it can be shown that it will result in some immediate and substantial benefit to the injured person which would not otherwise accrue if the funds remained under the control of the court. It should be noted that money held by the court is disregarded for benefit purposes, so that it is not necessary for a trust to be created to shelter the money if the injured person is in receipt of income based benefits, and the Court of Protection therefore does not consider it necessary for a trust to be created in all cases. The main question is whether the injured person will benefit as a result of the trust, and the application to the court should therefore outline the benefits to the injured person as clearly as possible.

Because the Court of Protection is giving up control over the funds by allowing the setting up of a private personal injury trust, it is reluctant to agree to a trust such as a discretionary trust where control is vested entirely in the hands of the trustees. The court will normally require a bare trust instead. There must be a professional trustee with relevant experience, and this must be shown.

Usually the trust will provide on death any remaining assets within the trust are paid to the injured person's personal representatives.

The court may retain control over certain aspects of the trust, such as the distribution of capital, and reserve the right to approve the appointment of new trustees.

In many cases the deputy will be discharged following the setting up of the trust, but in other cases the retention may be desirable for other purposes.

CHAPTER TEN
PROBLEM AREAS FOR PRACTITIONERS

10.1 Fatalities Cases

If the injured person dies before the claim is settled, any compensation will be due to their estate. This cannot be sheltered under the benefits rules referred to above, and it may therefore be the outcome that the surviving spouse is unable to claim means tested benefits because of the amount of capital inherited.

This was confirmed in commissioners decision **R(IS) 3/03**, where a widow was paid for a claim under the **Fatal Accidents Act 1976**. For the purposes of entitlement to income support, HHJ Turnbull held that, although the money had been paid into a personal injury trust, it would not be disregarded as she had not herself suffered the injury.

Other means tested benefit rules, such as the pension credit regulations, and indeed the Care Act regulations, are worded slightly differently and might offer some scope for negotiation. However, it seems likely that a commissioner or court interpreting the matter would give a purposive interpretation to the legislation and would interpret it in order to be in line with the income support regulations.

It should also be mentioned that references to 'partner' in the legislation refer to living partners and therefore do not apply in cases where one partner has already died.

There are two possibilities for dealing with such a case. The first is to take advantage of existing benefits disregards, in particular the disregard for the value of the family home. It would be possible to pay to purchase a home, or indeed an improved one, with the capital, and thereby avoid its being taken into account. There are also other possible items of expenditure which may help to shelter some of the capital, although the rules on deprivation outlined above in Chapter 4.2 should be considered. However, it is worth noting that the deprivation rule will not apply to a conversion of a disregarded capital asset into another disregarded capital asset.

There is an alternative which may arise in a case where the defendant is a body such as the CICA or the MIB. In such cases the defendant may agree to act as settlor and to pay the money into a discretionary trust. In this case the argument would be that the survivor will never receive the funds outright. This is by no means certain to work, but may be worth a try.

10.2 Professional Negligence

In cases in which solicitors have failed correctly to plead a claim for personal injury, or to do so in time, so that the injured party has been unable to recover the full amount of his or her claim directly from the other party or the insurers, it may be possible to sue the solicitors for professional negligence. If such a claim succeeds, are the proceeds of that claim payments made in consequence of personal injury, and therefore capable of being paid into the trust? Since the payments are made in consequence of the personal injury to the claimant, the Upper Tribunal in **KQ v SSWP (IS) [2011] UKUT 102 (AAC)** held that they were so capable.

In passing, it is worth noting that the wording used is not 'compensation awarded' but 'payment made'. There may therefore be scope for other types of payment, such as payments from insurance policies or ill health retirement payments, to be validly placed into a personal injury trust. However, the DWP may take a different view.

10.3 Past Care Awards

In many cases, an element of an award of compensation will be for 'past (or gratuitous) care' which has already been provided to the injured person by friends or family. An award of damages may in part reflect their contribution, and under the rule in **Hunt v Severs [1994] 2 AC 350**, the claimant holds that part of his or her damages which reflect the cost of that care in trust for the carer.

If the carers are the spouse or family of the injured party, and if such a sum becomes available to them, then it will be a change of circumstances and may affect their entitlement to means tested benefits. If the injured person is a child, then he or she will not be the benefits claimant at all, and it is most likely that the claimant will be the parent. The issue is whether the money paid will take the claiming unit over the threshold. The Court of Appeal in **Peters** (see Chapter 7.3) held that the whole of an award was disregarded for the purposes of local authority-brokered care except for the cost of care, which is only disregarded if the award is held in a PI trust or administered by a court.

There are two alternative approaches to such a situation. One is to argue that the payment is in itself a payment made in consequence of a personal injury to the claimant, and that it can therefore be settled into a personal injury trust. The alternative approach, which comes to a different conclusion, is that the past care award is attributable to care by a third party and is payable to the person who provided the care. If the carer is a member of the same claimant unit, however, this will in effect mean that the money is nevertheless theirs, even if it is placed in the PI trust.

To avoid ambiguity and confusion it is worth detailing the care award as a separate item of damages.

Any capital so paid, if it cannot be paid into a trust as suggested above, cannot be sheltered by the use of the rules as to disregards discussed here, and it may therefore be advisable to look at other ways of dealing with such money, such as purchase of or improvement of a house as outlined above.

10.4 Divorce

This raises the question whether, in the event of a divorce where there is already a personal injury trust in place, the money in the trust is 'up for grabs'. The court has power under Section 24 of the **Matrimonial Causes Act 1973** to vary both ante-nuptial and post-nuptial settlements, and the personal injury trust may well fall within that definition. If it is to be an ante-nuptial settlement, it must be made in contemplation of marriage. Since such a trust is likely to make provision for the spouse and/or all children in any event, such an arrangement may well fall within **Section 24**. Children may also bring a claim under **Section 24**.

Even if the trust is a bare trust, the court has power under **Section 37** of the **Matrimonial Causes Act 1973** to set aside the personal injury trust if they consider that it was effected to reduce or impede a claim for financial relief by a spouse.

The important question is what the settlor intended. Within 3 years of setting up the trust, there is a presumption that the setting up of the trust was intended to defeat a claim for financial relief. If actual intention can be shown, that time limit can be extended.

The counter argument is likely to be that the presumption fails, since the trust was set up in order to maintain means tested benefits.

The money is also likely to be kept separate from any other assets of the injured party, and this may well be useful in persuading the judge that the money is intended for the benefit of the settlor only.

Another possibility which should be born in mind is that the injury to one party in a family may well have significant and on-going effects on other members of the family. For example, a spouse may give up work to look after their injured spouse full time. The result would be a drop in the standard living of the family.

It is important to note the trends within the courts for dealing with such arrangements, moving away from evidence of who contributed the majority of money in a case where the marriage has subsisted for a long time. This follows from the case of **White v White [2000] 2 FLR 981**.

Retirement provision is a further consideration. There are now provisions for pension sharing on divorce, and there is generally a greater awareness of the effects of divorce on the old age of both parties. A spouse who has given up work to care full time for an injured spouse may well not have been able to save money for his or her own retirement, and this is a matter which the court may take into account.

In the event of a divorce, it has to be accepted that a personal injury trust may not succeed in protecting the money. It may, however, help to delineate which of the assets are personal injury trust assets.

10.5 Disagreement among the Trustees

Trustees are required to act unanimously, and a decision cannot be taken if one of them is not in agreement with the others. This can cause problems, particularly where trustees may be family members. On the occasions when there is a dispute within the family, this may create an issue which has to be addressed with regard to the trust.

The question is often more straightforward if the settlor is mentally capable. This is because the settlor will normally retain to him or herself the power of appointing new trustees, and can simply deal with the matter by removing the recalcitrant trustee(s) and replacing them. If the settlor does not have capacity, however, it may be necessary for one or other of the trustees to seek directions from the court. The official solicitor may have to act for the settlor in the application.

In one case drawn to the author's attention, professional trustees applied for directions, and also for the removal of a family trustee. Financial advisors had advised that the resources of the compensated person were being spent far too rapidly, and these would run out before the expected termination of the settlor's life. The professional trustees also harboured a suspicion that money was being spent for the maintenance of a family as a whole, and not simply for the disabled person and their carers. Unfortunately the compensated person died before the case could be heard.

It is important within the trust not to lose sight of the question of whom the money actually belongs to. Where there are family trustees, the resources of the compensated person and the trustees do tend to become intermixed, both as a result of property transactions such as those necessary to fund a more suitable property, and as a result of the payment of support payments to enable carers to stay at home and provide the care.

10.6 Death of the Settlor

On death of the settlor, subject to the remarks above, a capital gains tax free uplift will apply, so that any gains obtained during the settlor's lifetime will not attract CGT. Inheritance tax will normally be payable on the estate at a rate of 40% of the excess over the amount of the nil rate band, which is currently £325,000.

10.6.1 Bare Trusts

On the settlor's death, the assets will fall into the settlor's estate and will be **distributed in accordance with the testator's Will or the intestacy rules.** **Note** should be taken of the potential effect on recipients of means tested benefits, and planning measures put in place in case this is likely to be an issue. This may also be relevant in a case of, for example, an impending divorce.

The assets of the trust form part of the settlor's estate and are taxable accordingly if the nil rate band is exceeded.

10.6.2 Flexible Life Interest Trusts

The assets of the trust will form part of the settlor's estate because of the reservation of benefit rules, whether it was set up before or after March 2006. The assets in a life interest trust and the assets in the settlor's other estate will each receive a proportion of the deceased's nil rate band for inheritance tax purposes.

10.6.3 Discretionary Trusts

The death of the settlor triggers an inheritance tax charge because the settlement of personal injury compensation into a discretionary trust of which a person is a beneficiary would count as a 'gift with reservation'. The value of the assets is treated as part of the settlor's estate for inheritance tax purposes. If the settlor is another person, it may be possible to avoid this, but HMRC will look closely at it. The assets in the trust, and the deceased's other estate, will share the nil rate band as above.

10.6.4 Trusts for Mentally Capable Minors

A trust set up under CPR 21.11 is a bare trust and the funds are distributed in accordance with the Will or the intestacy rules. Note should be taken of the possibility that the intestacy rules will permit inheritance by a parent who is responsible for the injuries to their child. This cannot be avoided with a bare trust, but for example the CICA will insist on the trust not being established as a bare trust for that reason. Where a person is over 18 a Will is essential.

10.6.5 Section 89 Trusts for a Disabled Person

These settlements suffer from the same 'gifts with reservations' problems as an ordinary discretionary or life interest trust. If the trust is discretionary, then the trustees can distribute to the eventual beneficiaries or, if they prefer, keep the trust in existence. Inheritance tax is payable proportionately from the deceased's estate on the assets in the trust and the other assets.

10.6.6 General Considerations

10.6.6.1 Beneficiaries

Where beneficiaries under a Will or under the intestacy rules are receiving or likely to receive means tested benefits, then the effect of the death of the settlor on their continuing right to receive benefits should be noted. A discretionary trust may be a good way of avoiding this problem.

If the chosen beneficiary is unable to deal with their own money themselves, for whatever reason, then the discretionary or life interest trust may be useful. Where there are reasons for not allowing a beneficiary to receive and control the money outright, for example because of business dealings or because of their marital situation, then a discretionary or life interest trust under the Will of the compensated person should also be considered.

If the compensated person can decide on the potential beneficiaries, but not on the proportions that they should receive, the solution may be to set up a discretionary will trust with a letter of wishes. This can be changed later. This is also a way of dealing with the future circumstances of the beneficiaries which may at present be unknown.

Consideration should be given to the identity of the proposed executors. Where there is a professional trustee of the lifetime trust, it may be appropriate for this to continue. Dealing over a period of time with a continuing trust can be a difficult task, and can be easier with a professional trustee. Being a continuing trustee is a slightly different situation from being an executor, where the winding up of the estate is a finite process.

It should be noted that mental capacity rules are issue specific. This means that, although the compensated person may not be mentally capable of dealing with their own financial affairs, they may nevertheless be capable of making a Will (see for example **A, B and C v X and Z [2012] EWHC 2400**). If they are not, then consideration should be given to applying for a statutory will under **section 18** of the **Mental Capacity Act 2005**.

Where part of the proceeds of the compensation have been used to purchase or to adapt a property for the occupation of the injured person, consideration should be given to the position of the carers on the death of the injured person. This is particularly so if carers have given up their own homes to come to care full time for the disabled person. Some sort of arrangement, such as a life interest or discretionary trust, needs to be put in place to ensure that the carers are not faced with the loss of their home on the death of the settlor.

The compensation is intended to care for the injured person, and not as an asset to be disposed of on death. However, it is important that a Will should be made, and also that consideration to appropriate forms of inheritance tax planning, such as taking advantage of the spousal exemption. The life expectancy of a spouse of an injured person can be quite different from that of the injured person themselves.

10.6.6.2 Deaths of Other People

Where a personal injury trust has been set up in order to preserve the settlor's means tested benefits, consideration should be given as to the position if another person were to die and leave a capital sum to the settlor. This cannot be placed in the personal injury trust since it is not payment in respect of the injury, even if the testator expresses in his or her Will the view that they are making provision for the person for that reason. It may therefore be necessary to consider whether another form of trust should be set up, such as a Section 89 trust. A deed of variation entered into by the injured person may well be considered to be deprivation of capital for the purpose of the benefit rules. A further problem which may occur is where the person who dies is the owner or co-owner of the home of where the injured person lives. Consideration may need to be given to the possibility of the trust buying out the deceased owner's share if that is possible.

In the event of the death of one or more trustees, then consideration must be given to the powers within the trust as to who may appoint new trustees. If this is the settlor under a bare trust, then this is a straight forward process. In other forms of trust, it may be for the surviving trustees to appoint. If any of the appointers is themselves mentally incapable, then an order of the court will be required to allow the signature on the deed of appointment.

CHAPTER ELEVEN
CONCLUSION AND FURTHER RESOURCES

Personal injury trusts have developed significantly since the changes to the benefit regulations. In the absence of complications (such as incapacity, or inheritance tax problems) there is no reason, in most cases, why a trust should not be created in most situations, which in view of the wide definition of personal injury compensation, need not be confined to the commonly recognised forms of personal injury attracting compensation through actions for negligence. In the majority of cases, a bare trust will suffice to meet the needs of the benefit legislation, and also to provide other advantages depending on the particular circumstances. Even if there are complications such as incapacity or minority, the Court of Protection, or the High Court in the case of a mentally capable minor, is usually ready to assist with the appropriate arrangements.

However, the potential complexities must not be ignored, especially where tax considerations intervene; and the benefit complications mentioned in the preface must also be kept in mind. With that in view, there are two works to which attention should be drawn as providing additional help.

The first is Coldrick on Personal Injury Trusts (4th edition, Ark Publications, 2008). This very comprehensive work also contains useful advice about developing the work of a firm in providing the service of personal injury trusts. Its problem now is its age, but it nevertheless remains (if approached with care) a useful work of reference. The other is the

Welfare Benefits and Tax Credits Handbook 2020/21, published annually by the Child Poverty Action Group. This is a quite invaluable guide through the complexities of benefit law. Child Poverty Action Group website is also a valuable source of information and other resources, particularly with regard to Universal Credit (http://www.cpag.org.uk)

APPENDIX 1

ASSESSMENT FOR PERSONAL INDEPENDENCE PAYMENTS

1. Daily Living Activities	
Preparing food	**Pts**
a. Can prepare and cook a simple meal unaided	0
b. Needs to use an aid or appliance to be able to either prepare or cook a simple meal	2
c. cannot cook a simple meal using a conventional cooker but is able to do so using a microwave	2
d. needs prompting to be able to either prepare or cook a simple meal	2
e. needs supervision or assistance to either prepare or cook a simple meal	4
f. cannot prepare and cook food	8
Taking nutrition	
a. Can take nutrition unaided.	0
b. Needs – (i) to use an aid or appliance to be able to take nutrition; or (ii) supervision to be able to take nutrition; or (iii) assistance to be able to cut up food.	2
c. Needs a therapeutic source to be able to take nutrition.	2
d. Needs prompting to be able to take nutrition.	4
e. Needs assistance to be able to manage a therapeutic source to take nutrition.	6

f. Cannot convey food and drink to their mouth and needs another person to do so.10	10
Managing therapy or monitoring a health condition	
a. Either – (i) does not receive medication or therapy or need to monitor a health condition; or (ii) can manage medication or therapy or monitor a health condition unaided.	0
b. Needs either – (i) to use an aid or appliance to be able to manage medication; or (ii) supervision, prompting or assistance to be able to manage medication or monitor a health condition.	1
c. Needs supervision, prompting or assistance to be able to manage therapy that takes no more than 3.5 hours a week.	2
d. Needs supervision, prompting or assistance to be able to manage therapy that takes more than 3.5 but no more than 7 hours a week.	4
e. Needs supervision, prompting or assistance to be able to manage therapy that takes more than 7 but no more than 14 hours a week.	6
f. Needs supervision, prompting or assistance to be able to manage therapy that takes more than 14 hours a week.	8
Washing and bathing.	
a. Can wash and bathe unaided.	0
b. Needs to use an aid or appliance to be able to wash or bathe.	2
c. Needs supervision or prompting to be able to wash or bathe.	2
d. Needs assistance to be able to wash either their hair or body below the waist.	2
e. Needs assistance to be able to get in or out of a bath or shower.	3

f. Needs assistance to be able to wash their body between the shoulders and waist.	4
g. Cannot wash and bathe at all and needs another person to wash their entire body.	8
Managing toilet needs or incontinence.	
a. Can manage toilet needs or incontinence unaided.	0
b. Needs to use an aid or appliance to be able to manage toilet needs or incontinence.	2
c. Needs supervision or prompting to be able to manage toilet needs.	2
d. Needs assistance to be able to manage toilet needs.	4
e. Needs assistance to be able to manage incontinence of either bladder or bowel.	6
f. Needs assistance to be able to manage incontinence of both bladder and bowel.	8
Dressing and undressing.	
a. Can dress and undress unaided.	0
b. Needs to use an aid or appliance to be able to dress or undress.	2
c. Needs either - (i) prompting to be able to dress, undress or determine appropriate circumstances for remaining clothed; or (ii) prompting or assistance to be able to select appropriate clothing.	2
d. Needs assistance to be able to dress or undress their lower body.	2
e. Needs assistance to be able to dress or undress their upper body.	4
f. Cannot dress or undress at all.	8

Communicating verbally.	
a. Can express and understand verbal information unaided.	0
b. Needs to use an aid or appliance to be able to speak or hear.	2
c. Needs communication support to be able to express or understand complex verbal information.	4
d. Needs communication support to be able to express or understand basic verbal information.	8
e. Cannot express or understand verbal information at all even with communication support.	12
8. Reading and understanding signs, symbols and words.	
a. Can read and understand basic and complex written information either unaided or using spectacles or contact lenses.	0
b. Needs to use an aid or appliance, other than spectacles or contact lenses, to be able to read or understand either basic or complex written information.	2
c. Needs prompting to be able to read or understand complex written information.	2
d. Needs prompting to be able to read or understand basic written information.	4
e. Cannot read or understand signs, symbols or words at all.	8
9. Engaging with other people face to face.	
a. Can engage with other people unaided.	0
b. Needs prompting to be able to engage with other people.	2
c. Needs social support to be able to engage with other people.	4
d. Cannot engage with other people due to such engagement causing either – (i) overwhelming psychological distress to the claimant; or	8

(ii) the claimant to exhibit behaviour which would result in a substantial risk of harm to the claimant or another person.	
10. Making budgeting decisions.	
a. Can manage complex budgeting decisions unaided.	0
b. Needs prompting or assistance to be able to make complex budgeting decisions.	2
c. Needs prompting or assistance to be able to make simple budgeting decisions.	4
d. Cannot make any budgeting decisions at all.	6
2. Mobility Activities	
1. Planning and following journeys	
a. Can plan and follow the route of a journey unaided.	0
b. Needs prompting to be able to undertake any journey to avoid overwhelming psychological distress to the claimant.	4
c. Cannot plan the route of a journey.	8
d. Cannot follow the route of an unfamiliar journey without another person, assistance dog or orientation aid.	10
e. Cannot undertake any journey because it would cause overwhelming psychological distress to the claimant.	12
f. Cannot follow the route of a familiar journey without another person, an assistance dog or an orientation aid.	12
2. Moving around	
a. Can stand and then move more than 200 metres, either aided or unaided.	0

b. Can stand and then move more than 50 metres but no more than 200 metres, either aided or unaided	4
c. Can stand and then move unaided more than 20 metres but no more than 50 metres.	8
d. Can stand and then move using an aid or appliance more than 20 metres but no more than 50 metres.	10
e. Can stand and then move more than 1 metre but no more than 20 metres, either aided or unaided.	12
f. Cannot, either aided or unaided, – (i) stand; or (ii) move more than 1 metre.	12

Source: Social Security (Personal Independence Payment) Regs 2013 No 377, First Schedule.

APPENDIX 2

EMPLOYMENT AND SUPPORT ALLOWANCE

ESA replaced incapacity benefit as the main benefit for someone who was unable to work owing to sickness or disability. Rather than assessing ability to work by way of an individual medical examination, ESA proceeds on the basis that, for a person to be entitled to the benefit, he or she must firstly have limited capability for work. That is determined by reference to the table below. In order to be considered to have limited capability for work, and thus to qualify, the claimant must have at least 15 points from one or more of the situations below. The law is found in the Employment and Support Allowance Regulations 2013 Schedule 2.

ASSESSMENT OF WHETHER A CLAIMANT HAS LIMITED CAPABILITY FOR WORK

Part 1 Physical disabilities

Activity	*Descriptors*		*Pts*
1. Mobilising unaided by another person with or without a walking stick, manual wheelchair or other aid if such aid can reasonably be used.	(a)	Cannot, unaided by another person, either: (i) mobilise more than 50 metres on level ground without stopping in order to avoid significant discomfort or exhaustion; or	15

		(ii) repeatedly mobilise 50 metres within a reasonable timescale because of significant discomfort or exhaustion.	
	(b)	Cannot mount or descend two steps unaided by another person even with the support of a handrail.	9
	(c)	Cannot, unaided by another person, either: (i) mobilise more than 100 metres on level ground without stopping in order to avoid significant discomfort or exhaustion; or (ii) repeatedly mobilise 100 metres within a reasonable timescale because of significant discomfort or exhaustion.	9
	(d)	Cannot, unaided by another person, either: (i) mobilise more than 200 metres on level ground without stopping in order to avoid significant discomfort or exhaustion; or (ii) repeatedly mobilise 200 metres within a reasonable timescale because of significant discomfort or exhaustion.	6
	(e)	None of the above apply.	0

2. Standing and sitting.	(a)	Cannot move between one seated position and another seated position located next to one another without receiving physical assistance from another person.	15
	(b)	Cannot, for the majority of the time, remain at a work station, either: (i) standing unassisted by another person (even if free to move around); or (ii) sitting (even in an adjustable chair) for more than 30 minutes, before needing to move away in order to avoid significant discomfort or exhaustion.	9
	(c)	Cannot, for the majority of the time, remain at a work station, either: (i) standing unassisted by another person (even if free to move around); (ii) sitting (even in an adjustable chair); or (iii) a combination of paragraphs (i) and (ii) for more than an hour before needing to move away in order to avoid significant discomfort or exhaustion.	6
	(d)	None of the above apply	0
3. Reaching.	(a)	Cannot raise either arm as if to put something in the top pocket of a coat or jacket.	15

	(b)	Cannot raise either arm to top of head as if to put on a hat.	9
	(c)	Cannot raise either arm above head height as if to reach for something.	6
	(d)	None of the above apply.	0
4. Picking up and moving or transferring by the use of the upper body and arms.	(a)	Cannot pick up and move a 0.5 litre carton full of liquid.	15
	(b)	Cannot pick up and move a one litre carton full of liquid.	9
	(c)	Cannot transfer a light but bulky object such as an empty cardboard box.	6
	(d)	None of the above apply.	0
5. Manual dexterity.	(a)	Cannot either: (i) press a button, such as a telephone keypad; or (ii) turn the pages of a book with either hand.	15
	(b)	Cannot pick up a £1 coin or equivalent with either hand.	15
	(c)	Cannot use a pen or pencil to make a meaningful mark.	9
	(d)	Cannot use a suitable keyboard or mouse.	9
	(e)	None of the above apply.	0
6. Making self understood through speaking, writing, typing, or other	(a)	Cannot convey a simple message, such as the presence of a hazard.	15
	(b)	Has significant difficulty conveying a simple message to strangers.	15

means normally used, unaided by another person.	(c)	Has some difficulty conveying a simple message to strangers.	6
	(d)	None of the above apply.	0
7. Understanding communication by (i) verbal means (such as hearing or lip reading) alone; (ii) non-verbal means (such as reading 16 point print or Braille) alone; or (iii) a combination of sub-paragraphs (i) and (ii) using any aid that is normally or could reasonably be used, unaided by another person.	(a)	Cannot understand a simple message due to sensory impairment, such as the location of a fire escape.	15
	(b)	Has significant difficulty understanding a simple message from a stranger due to sensory impairment.	15
	(c)	Has some difficulty understanding a simple message from a stranger due to sensory impairment.	6
	(d)	None of the above apply.	0
8. Navigation and maintaining safety, using a guide dog or other aid if normally used.	(a)	Unable to navigate around familiar surroundings, without being accompanied by another person, due to sensory impairment.	15
	(b)	Cannot safely complete a potentially hazardous task such as crossing the road, without being accompanied by another person, due to sensory impairment.	15
	(c)	Unable to navigate around unfamiliar surroundings, without being accompanied by another person, due to sensory impairment.	9
	(d)	None of the above apply.	0

9. Absence or loss of control while conscious leading to extensive evacuation of the bowel and/or bladder, other than enuresis (bed-wetting) despite the wearing or use of any aids or adaptations which are normally or could reasonably be worn or used.	(a)	At least once a month experiences: (i) loss of control leading to extensive evacuation of the bowel and/or voiding of the bladder; or (ii) substantial leakage of the contents of a collecting device sufficient to require cleaning and a change in clothing.	15
	(b)	The majority of the time is at risk of loss of control leading to extensive evacuation of the bowel and/or voiding of the bladder, sufficient to require cleaning and a change in clothing, if not able to reach a toilet quickly.	6
	(c)	None of the above apply.	0
10. Consciousness during waking moments.	(a)	At least once a week, has an nvoluntary episode of lost or altered consciousness resulting in significantly disrupted awareness or concentration.	15
	(b)	At least once a month, has an involuntary episode of lost or altered consciousness resulting in significantly disrupted awareness or concentration.	6
	(c)	None of the above apply.	0.

Part 2 Mental, cognitive and intellectual function assessment

11. Learning tasks.	(a)	Cannot learn how to complete a simple task, such as setting an alarm clock.	15
	(b)	Cannot learn anything beyond a simple task, such as setting an alarm clock.	9
	(c)	Cannot learn anything beyond a moderately complex task, such as the steps involved in operating a washing machine to clean clothes.	6
	(d)	None of the above apply.	0
12. Awareness of everyday hazards (such as boiling water or sharp objects).	(a)	Reduced awareness of everyday hazards leads to a significant risk of: (i) injury to self or others; or (ii) damage to property or possessions such that they require supervision for the majority of the time to maintain safety.	15
	(b)	Reduced awareness of everyday hazards leads to a significant risk of (i) injury to self or others; or (ii) damage to property or possessions such that they frequently require supervision to maintain safety.	9
	(c)	Reduced awareness of everyday hazards leads to a significant risk of:	6

		(i) injury to self or others; or (ii) damage to property or possessions such that they occasionally require supervision to maintain safety.	
	(d)	None of the above apply.	0
13. Initiating and completing personal action (which means planning, organisation, problem solving, prioritising or switching tasks).	(a)	Cannot, due to impaired mental function, reliably initiate or complete at least 2 sequential personal actions.	15
	(b)	Cannot, due to impaired mental function, reliably initiate or complete at least 2 personal actions for the majority of the time.	9
	(c)	Frequently cannot, due to impaired mental function, reliably initiate or complete at least 2 personal actions.	6
	(d)	None of the above apply.	0
14. Coping with change.	(a)	Cannot cope with any change to the extent that day to day life cannot be managed.	15
	(b)	Cannot cope with minor planned change (such as a pre-arranged change to the routine time scheduled for a lunch break), to the extent that overall day to day life is made significantly more difficult.	9
	(c)	Cannot cope with minor unplanned change (such as the timing of an appointment on the day it is due to occur), to the extent that overall, day to day life is made significantly more difficult.	6

	(d)	None of the above apply.	0
15. Getting about.	(a)	Cannot get to any specified place with which the claimant is familiar.	15
	(b)	Is unable to get to a specified place with which the claimant is familiar, without being accompanied by another person.	9
	(c)	Is unable to get to a specified place with which the claimant is unfamiliar without being accompanied by another person.	6
	(d)	None of the above apply.	0
16. Coping with social engagement due to cognitive impairment or mental disorder.	(a)	Engagement in social contact is always precluded due to difficulty relating to others or significant distress experienced by the individual.	15
	(b)	Engagement in social contact with someone unfamiliar to the claimant is always precluded due to difficulty relating to others or significant distress experienced by the individual.	9
	(c)	Engagement in social contact with someone unfamiliar to the claimant is not possible for the majority of the time due to difficulty relating to others or significant distress experienced by the individual.	6
	(d)	None of the above apply.	0
17. Appropriateness of behaviour with other people, due to cognitive impairment	(a)	Has, on a daily basis, uncontrollable episodes of aggressive or disinhibited behaviour that would be unreasonable in any workplace.	15

or mental disorder.	(b)	Frequently has uncontrollable episodes of aggressive or disinhibited behaviour that would be unreasonable in any workplace.	15
	(c)	Occasionally has uncontrollable episodes of aggressive or disinhibited behaviour that would be unreasonable in any workplace.	9
	(d)	None of the above apply.	0

Assuming the claimant qualifies, he or she will be entitled to benefit at a standard rate for the first 13 weeks (usually) of the claim (known as the assessment phase). During 2020/21 this rate is £73.10 per week, plus any premiums for which the claimant qualifies. Once the assessment phase ends, he or she will receive the basic allowance plus an additional component depending on whether he or she also has "limited capability for work-related activity". This is determined by reference to the table below (although certain people qualify automatically). If the claimant fulfils one or more of the conditions below for (generally) fifty percent of their time, they are deemed to be in the "support group" and paid an additional component of £38.55 a week. If they do not fulfil the criteria below, they are in the "work-related activity group" and receive an additional component of £29.05 a week, and are also required to take steps to look for work which they might do.

ASSESSMENT OF WHETHER A CLAIMANT HAS LIMITED CAPABILITY FOR WORK RELATED ACTIVITY

Activity	*Descriptors*
1. Mobilising unaided by another person with or without a walking stick, manual wheelchair or other aid if such aid can reasonably be used.	Cannot either: (a) mobilise more than 50 metres on level ground without stopping in order to avoid significant discomfort or exhaustion; or (b) repeatedly mobilise 50 metres within a reasonable timescale because of significant discomfort or exhaustion.
2. Transferring from one seated position to another.	Cannot move between one seated position and another seated position located next to one another without receiving physical assistance from another person.
3. Reaching.	Cannot raise either arm as if to put something in the top pocket of a coat or jacket.
4. Picking up and moving or transferring by the use of the upper body and arms (excluding standing, sitting, bending or kneeling and all other activities specified in this Schedule).	Cannot pick up and move a 0.5 litre carton full of liquid.

5. Manual dexterity.	Cannot either: (a) press a button, such as a telephone keypad; or (b) turn the pages of a book with either hand.
6. Making self understood through speaking, writing, typing, or other means normally used.	Cannot convey a simple message, such as the presence of a hazard.
7. Understanding communication by (i) verbal means (such as hearing or lip reading) alone; (ii) non-verbal means (such as reading 16 point print or Braille) alone; or (iii) a combination of sub-paragraphs (i) and (ii) using any aid that is normally, or could reasonably, be used unaided by another person.	Cannot understand a simple message due to sensory impairment, such as the location of a fire escape.
8. Absence or loss of control over extensive evacuation of the bowel and/or voiding of the bladder, other than enuresis (bed-wetting), despite the presence of any aids or adaptations normally used.	At least once a week experiences: (a) loss of control leading to extensive evacuation of the bowel and/or voiding of the bladder; or (b) substantial leakage of the contents of a collecting device sufficient to require the individual to clean themselves and change clothing.

9. Learning tasks.	Cannot learn how to complete a simple task, such as setting an alarm clock, due to cognitive impairment or mental disorder.
10. Awareness of hazard.	Reduced awareness of everyday hazards, due to cognitive impairment or mental disorder, leads to a significant risk of: (a) injury to self or others; or (b) damage to property or possessions such that they require supervision for the majority of the time to maintain safety.
11. Initiating and completing personal action (which means planning, organisation, problem solving, prioritising or switching tasks).	Cannot, due to impaired mental function, reliably initiate or complete at least 2 sequential personal actions.
12. Coping with change.	Cannot cope with any change, due to cognitive impairment or mental disorder, to the extent that day to day life cannot be managed.
13. Coping with social engagement, due to cognitive impairment or mental disorder.	Engagement in social contact is always precluded due to difficulty relating to others or significant distress experienced by the individual.
14. Appropriateness of behaviour with other people, due to cognitive impairment or mental disorder.	Has, on a daily basis, uncontrollable episodes of aggressive or disinhibited behaviour that would be unreasonable in any workplace.

15. Conveying food or drink to the mouth.	(a)	Cannot convey food or drink to the claimant's own mouth without receiving physical assistance from someone else;		
	(b)	Cannot convey food or drink to the claimant's own mouth without repeatedly stopping, experiencing breathlessness or severe discomfort;		
	(c)	Cannot convey food or drink to the claimant's own mouth without receiving regular prompting given by someone else in the claimant's physical presence; or		
	(d)	Owing to a severe disorder of mood or behaviour, fails to convey food or drink to the claimant's own mouth without receiving:		
			(i)	physical assistance from someone else; or
			(ii)	regular prompting given by someone else in the claimant's pres-ence.
16. Chewing or swallowing food or drink.	(a)	Cannot chew or swallow food or drink;		

	(b)	Cannot chew or swallow food or drink without repeatedly stopping, experiencing breathlessness or severe discomfort;
	(c)	Cannot chew or swallow food or drink without repeatedly receiving regular prompting given by someone else in the claimant's presence; or
	(d)	Owing to a severe disorder of mood or behaviour, fails to: (i) chew or swallow food or drink; or (ii) chew or swallow food or drink without regular prompting given by someone else in the claimant's presence."

Source: Employment and Support Allowance Regulations 2013, Schedules 2 and 3, and the Universal Credit Regulations 2013 (where they are repeated), Schedules 6 and 7.

MORE BOOKS BY LAW BRIEF PUBLISHING

A selection of our other titles available now:-

'A Practical Guide to the General Data Protection Regulation (GDPR) – 2nd Edition' by Keith Markham
'Ellis on Credit Hire – Sixth Edition' by Aidan Ellis & Tim Kevan
'A Practical Guide to Working with Litigants in Person and McKenzie Friends in Family Cases' by Stuart Barlow
'Protecting Unregistered Brands: A Practical Guide to the Law of Passing Off' by Lorna Brazell
'A Practical Guide to Secondary Liability and Joint Enterprise Post-Jogee' by Joanne Cecil & James Mehigan
'A Practical Guide to the Pre-Action RTA Claims Protocol for Personal Injury Lawyers' by Antonia Ford
'A Practical Guide to Neighbour Disputes and the Law' by Alexander Walsh
'A Practical Guide to Forfeiture of Leases' by Mark Shelton
'A Practical Guide to Coercive Control for Legal Practitioners and Victims' by Rachel Horman
'A Practical Guide to Rights Over Airspace and Subsoil' by Daniel Gatty
'Tackling Disclosure in the Criminal Courts – A Practitioner's Guide' by Narita Bahra QC & Don Ramble
'A Practical Guide to the Law of Driverless Cars – Second Edition' by Alex Glassbrook, Emma Northey & Scarlett Milligan
'A Practical Guide to TOLATA Claims' by Greg Williams
'Artificial Intelligence – The Practical Legal Issues' by John Buyers
'A Practical Guide to the Law of Prescription in Scotland' by Andrew Foyle
'A Practical Guide to the Construction and Rectification of Wills and Trust Instruments' by Edward Hewitt
'A Practical Guide to the Law of Bullying and Harassment in the Workplace' by Philip Hyland

'How to Be a Freelance Solicitor: A Practical Guide to the SRA-Regulated Freelance Solicitor Model' by Paul Bennett
'A Practical Guide to Prison Injury Claims' by Malcolm Johnson
'A Practical Guide to the Small Claims Track' by Dominic Bright
'A Practical Guide to Advising Clients at the Police Station' by Colin Stephen McKeown-Beaumont
'A Practical Guide to Antisocial Behaviour Injunctions' by Iain Wightwick
'Practical Mediation: A Guide for Mediators, Advocates, Advisers, Lawyers, and Students in Civil, Commercial, Business, Property, Workplace, and Employment Cases' by Jonathan Dingle with John Sephton
'The Mini-Pupillage Workbook' by David Boyle
'A Practical Guide to Crofting Law' by Brian Inkster
'A Practical Guide to Spousal Maintenance' by Liz Cowell
'A Practical Guide to the Law of Domain Names and Cybersquatting' by Andrew Clemson
'A Practical Guide to the Law of Gender Pay Gap Reporting' by Harini Iyengar
'A Practical Guide to the Rights of Grandparents in Children Proceedings' by Stuart Barlow
'NHS Whistleblowing and the Law' by Joseph England
'Employment Law and the Gig Economy' by Nigel Mackay & Annie Powell
'A Practical Guide to Noise Induced Hearing Loss (NIHL) Claims' by Andrew Mckie, Ian Skeate, Gareth McAloon
'An Introduction to Beauty Negligence Claims – A Practical Guide for the Personal Injury Practitioner' by Greg Almond
'Intercompany Agreements for Transfer Pricing Compliance' by Paul Sutton
'Zen and the Art of Mediation' by Martin Plowman
'A Practical Guide to the SRA Principles, Individual and Law Firm Codes of Conduct 2019 – What Every Law Firm Needs to Know' by Paul Bennett
'A Practical Guide to Adoption for Family Lawyers' by Graham Pegg
'A Practical Guide to Industrial Disease Claims' by Andrew Mckie & Ian Skeate
'A Practical Guide to Redundancy' by Philip Hyland
'A Practical Guide to Vicarious Liability' by Mariel Irvine

'A Practical Guide to Applications for Landlord's Consent and Variation of Leases' by Mark Shelton
'A Practical Guide to Relief from Sanctions Post-Mitchell and Denton' by Peter Causton
'A Practical Guide to Equity Release for Advisors' by Paul Sams
'A Practical Guide to Unlawful Eviction and Harassment' by Stephanie Lovegrove
'A Practical Guide to the Law Relating to Food' by Ian Thomas
'A Practical Guide to Financial Services Claims' by Chris Hegarty
'The Law of Houses in Multiple Occupation: A Practical Guide to HMO Proceedings' by Julian Hunt
'A Practical Guide to Unlawful Eviction and Harassment' by Stephanie Lovegrove
'A Practical Guide to Solicitor and Client Costs' by Robin Dunne
'Occupiers, Highways and Defective Premises Claims: A Practical Guide Post-Jackson – 2nd Edition' by Andrew Mckie
'A Practical Guide to Financial Ombudsman Service Claims' by Adam Temple & Robert Scrivenor
'A Practical Guide to the Law of Enfranchisement and Lease Extension' by Paul Sams
'A Practical Guide to Marketing for Lawyers – 2nd Edition' by Catherine Bailey & Jennet Ingram
'A Practical Guide to Advising Schools on Employment Law' by Jonathan Holden
'A Practical Guide to Running Housing Disrepair and Cavity Wall Claims: 2nd Edition' by Andrew Mckie & Ian Skeate
'A Practical Guide to Holiday Sickness Claims – 2nd Edition' by Andrew Mckie & Ian Skeate
'Arguments and Tactics for Personal Injury and Clinical Negligence Claims' by Dorian Williams
'A Practical Guide to QOCS and Fundamental Dishonesty' by James Bentley
'A Practical Guide to Drone Law' by Rufus Ballaster, Andrew Firman, Eleanor Clot
'A Practical Guide to Compliance for Personal Injury Firms Working With Claims Management Companies' by Paul Bennett
'A Practical Guide to the Landlord and Tenant Act 1954: Commercial Tenancies' by Richard Hayes & David Sawtell

www.ingramcontent.com/pod-product-compliance
Ingram Content Group UK Ltd.
Pitfield, Milton Keynes, MK11 3LW, UK
UKHW021239300926
15471UKWH00013B/700

9 781912 687855